797,885 Books

are available to read at

www.ForgottenBooks.com

Forgotten Books' App
Available for mobile, tablet & eReader

ISBN 978-1-330-66799-6
PIBN 10089815

This book is a reproduction of an important historical work. Forgotten Books uses state-of-the-art technology to digitally reconstruct the work, preserving the original format whilst repairing imperfections present in the aged copy. In rare cases, an imperfection in the original, such as a blemish or missing page, may be replicated in our edition. We do, however, repair the vast majority of imperfections successfully; any imperfections that remain are intentionally left to preserve the state of such historical works.

Forgotten Books is a registered trademark of FB &c Ltd.
Copyright © 2017 FB &c Ltd.
FB &c Ltd, Dalton House, 60 Windsor Avenue, London, SW19 2RR.
Company number 08720141. Registered in England and Wales.

For support please visit www.forgottenbooks.com

1 MONTH OF FREE READING

at
www.ForgottenBooks.com

By purchasing this book you are eligible for one month membership to ForgottenBooks.com, giving you unlimited access to our entire collection of over 700,000 titles via our web site and mobile apps.

To claim your free month visit:
www.forgottenbooks.com/free89815

* Offer is valid for 45 days from date of purchase. Terms and conditions apply.

English
Français
Deutsche
Italiano
Español
Português

www.forgottenbooks.com

Mythology Photography **Fiction**
Fishing Christianity **Art** Cooking
Essays Buddhism Freemasonry
Medicine **Biology** Music **Ancient Egypt** Evolution Carpentry Physics
Dance Geology **Mathematics** Fitness
Shakespeare **Folklore** Yoga Marketing
Confidence Immortality Biographies
Poetry **Psychology** Witchcraft
Electronics Chemistry History **Law**
Accounting **Philosophy** Anthropology
Alchemy Drama Quantum Mechanics
Atheism Sexual Health **Ancient History**
Entrepreneurship Languages Sport
Paleontology Needlework Islam
Metaphysics Investment Archaeology
Parenting Statistics Criminology
Motivational

PHILOSOPHY AND EXPERIENCE.

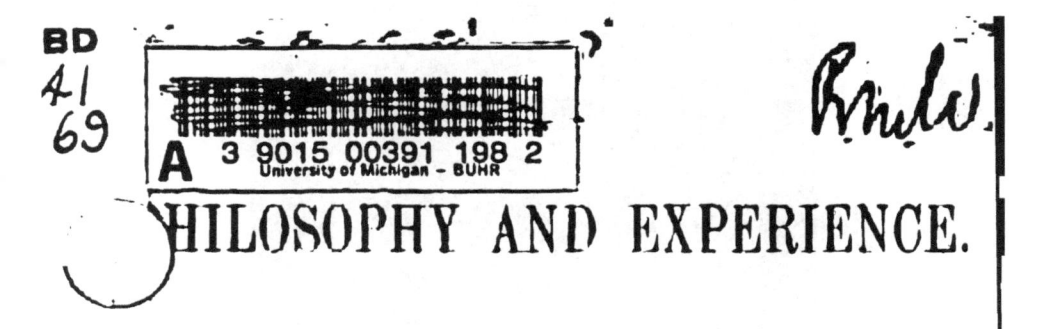

DELIVERED BEFORE THE ARISTOTELIAN SOCIETY,

OCTOBER 26, 1885

(BEING THE ANNUAL PRESIDENTIAL ADDRESS FOR THE SEVENTH
SESSION OF THE SOCIETY).

SHADWORTH H. HODGSON,

HONORARY LL.D. EDIN., HONORARY FELLOW OF C.C.C.

PRESIDENT.

ALL RIGHTS RESERVED.

PHILOSOPHY AND EXPERIENCE.

An Address

DELIVERED BEFORE THE ARISTOTELIAN SOCIETY,

OCTOBER 26, 1885

(BEING THE ANNUAL PRESIDENTIAL ADDRESS FOR THE SEVENTH
SESSION OF THE SOCIETY),

BY

SHADWORTH H. HODGSON,

HONORARY LL.D. EDIN., HONORARY FELLOW OF C.C.C. OXFORD,

PRESIDENT.

ALL RIGHTS RESERVED.

WILLIAMS AND NORGATE,
14 HENRIETTA STREET, COVENT GARDEN, LONDON;
AND 20 SOUTH FREDERICK STREET, EDINBURGH.
1885.

BD
41
.H69

PHILOSOPHY AND EXPERIENCE.

ONCE more we have met to kindle the sacred torch of philosophical enquiry among ourselves, and raise it if possible also as a witness to others, in a time which, whatever its degree of scientific enlightenment, has still but a vague, and perhaps on the whole even an unfavourable, conception of the nature, validity, and importance, of any method which is distinctly philosophical. Most people know and recognise common sense; many know and recognise science; few, very few in comparison, have any knowledge or appreciation of philosophy. What most people, it may be feared, understand by philosophising is simply indulging, by the light of nature, in ingenious speculations concerning the general purposes of creation.

In my remarks this evening, I wish to bring to some sort of completion that subject which has been the staple of my preceding Addresses, the subject of philosophical Method. Various sides and relations of philosophy have been brought forward in the course of those Addresses, but throughout there has run, as the guiding thread, the thought of Method, the consideration what the distinct mode of proceeding and enquiry must be, if Philosophy itself is to exist as an autonomous pursuit, if in short there be such a thing as Philosophy at all. This latter point was the one which I endeavoured, as you may remember, to establish in my first Address, chiefly by reference to the history of Philosophy. And the result I summed up in a brief phrase, not a definition but the foundation of one, to the effect, that the aim and purpose of Philosophy was to render the Universe of Things intelligible to thought, to give a *Rationale* of the Universe, so far as it was attainable by human powers. Thus I endeavoured to indicate, that the purpose of philosophy is to give systematic unity to human thought concerning the Universe, not necessarily to discover the principle or principles, the source or sources, from which the Universe proceeds. Whether this latter does or does not exceed human powers is a point for philosophy itself to determine.

In my second Address, "The Practical Bearing of Speculative Philosophy," the distinction between the two main branches of Philosophy, the speculative and the practical, was brought forward, and an answer drawn therefrom to the question, supposed to be propounded by a sceptic,—What, if any, was the good of Philosophy?

My third Address attacked the question of Method more directly, and from an analysis of the constant and essential feature in all distinct knowledge, that is to say, of the moment of Reflective Perception, called Apperception by Kant, elicited the fact, that all knowledge is knowledge because it contains, in its objects of whatever kind, the two contrasted but inseparable aspects of the *what* and the *that*, the nature of anything and the fact of its existence. And this, in combination with what had previously been said, led us to a formula defining philosophical method as—*subjective analysis of objects of consciousness by means of the distinction between conditions of their essence and conditions of their existence.*

My fourth Address was occupied with the further examination of this fundamental distinction of method, in connection with, and in the light of, the facts of experience to which it is applicable, and resulted in establishing two different senses in which we use the terms, real, objective, existent, and the like; the first sense denoting their simple perceivability, the simple fact of their existence, and the second sense denoting their foundation in, and dependence on, the laws which govern the order of nature, whether this order is or is not specifically known to us (See particularly pp. 30-33 of that Address). We thus obtain, it should be noted, a further specification and restriction of the term *real condition*, from the larger sense in which it covers both senses of reality, and in which it was used in the previous Address. A certain obscurity attaching to this twofold use of the term *real condition* and its congeners, which I am conscious of having left unremoved in my third Address, will, I hope, be completely dispelled by my remarks to-night, partly in consequence of the greater comprehensiveness of the present survey, partly perhaps of my own thought being now somewhat more definite and mature.

Lastly, in my Address of last year, the distinction between real conditioning, in this restricted sense, and the nature or essence of real objects, in the first sense of *reality*, was made the basis of drawing the line of demarcation between philosophy and science; philosophy, it was said, drawing the distinction, and thereby covering in some sort both domains, and at the same time assigning them severally, one to itself and the other to science, as their special provinces; that is to say, assigning to science all investigation of the order of real conditioning, whether in physics or in psychology, and retaining for itself all subjective analysis of essence, under which head falls, I may repeat, the drawing of the distinction itself. The term *philosophy* has thus both a broader and a narrower meaning. In the broader, it embraces all analysis of fact, including the fact of contrast between itself and science; in the narrower, it is analysis of fact, contrasted with the discovery of real conditions, which is the special province of science.

It is to philosophy in the broader sense that I wish to return to-night, as I hope my title *Philosophy and Experience* sufficiently indicates; to that broader sense which is contemplated by the phrase *Rationale of the Universe*, and also expressed by the definition of Method given in my third Address. The distinction between the two senses of *Reality*, which was drawn in my fourth Address, and upon which the distinction between philosophy and science was founded in my fifth, must itself be considered as a result obtained by applying the method as previously defined, that is, defined by means of the general distinction between conditions of essence and conditions of existence. I wish to-night to complete the outlines of this subject, by giving a sketch of the main departments into which philosophy is divisible; that is to say, of its organic articulation as a system of thought, in consequence of applying this same guiding distinction of method to the analysis of experience as a whole.

I.

[There* is no larger word than *Experience*. It is the equivalent of *Consciousness*. Kant defines it in several places by the phrase *empirisches Erkenntniss*, empirical knowledge. (E.g. in the Kritik d. R.V. Transcendental Deduction of the Categories, 2nd edit., p. 132 of Hartenstein's edition of 1853. Again in the same work, in the

---

* The part between brackets, the whole of Section I., down to the words *perfect comprehensiveness*, was omitted in delivery, and the following short transition substituted:—In proceeding to do this, it must be recalled in the first place, that experience, in the sense of *empirical knowledge*, Kant's "*empirisches Erkenntniss*," is alike our only basis and our only means of verification; secondly that, since in beginning to philosophise we find experience already in the form of a world of objects, as known to ordinary common sense, which are also the objects

Beweis of the *Analogien der Erfahrung*, p. 177. And again in the *Metaphysische Aufangsgründe der Naturwissenschaft*, Rosenkranz u. Schubert's edition of the *Werke*, vol. v. p. 312). It is in this alone that both the material and the verification of all our enquiries, and all our theorising, are found. Even if we ask, as Kant did, How experience itself is possible?—still the proofs, in support of whatever source or sources may be alleged transcending it, must be drawn from it, and have their own analogies in the experiential world. Except from experience we have in the last resort no means or materials for framing an hypothesis at all. But this is far from implying that error is impossible, or that experience is always in harmony with itself. When we try to harmonise different parts of our experience with each other, the main question is, whether by the experience which we take as our source, or by that which we take as our verification, we mean experiential data pure and simple, or on the contrary are giving the name of simple experience to data which are not pure and simple, but have passed through a transforming process in our minds, by means of arbitrary associations which have been forgotten. In the latter case, we are really treating unconscious assumptions as simple and undoubted facts of experience, their only true place in experience, did we but know it, being the category of errors.

---

investigated by positive science, philosophy necessarily comes forward as a third way of regarding the objective world, and presupposes the two other ways of common sense and positive science. Lastly it must be borne in mind, that philosophy is not merely a Theory of Knowledge (*Erkenntnisstheorie*), but a Theory, or rather, to use a less ambitious word, let us say a *conspectus* or general view, of Knowledge and its Objects together, a general view taken of Being in the largest sense. These are preliminaries on which I would gladly dwell at greater length, if time permitted. As it is, I hasten to my main theme.

A distrust of hypotheses on the ground of the extreme difficulty of obtaining experience in its ultimate simplicity, or lowest terms, unmixed with imagination, has been very frequent and prominent among Englishmen. If there is, properly speaking, an English School of philosophy at all, this distrust of hypothesis, and the consequent tendency to appeal to experience alone, would be its distinguishing characteristic. Consider the names of Bacon, Hobbes, Locke, Berkeley, Butler, Tucker, Hartley, Hume, the Mills, John Grote, G. H. Lewes. Amid all their differences, all their antagonisms, this insistance on experience, and experience alone, is common to them all. The Platonising philosophers must be placed in an opposite category, Henry More, Cudworth, Taylor, and others. Also it must be noted, that with Bentham and Coleridge, who, as J. S. Mill has remarked, were the two leading minds in philosophical thought in England, at the end of the last and beginning of the present century, there occurs a break in the tradition. Bentham's powerful but partial treatment of Ethic, from a law-reformer's point of view, had the effect of keeping in the background its dependence upon the analysis of human consciousness in its whole range, and thereby obscuring for a time the importance of that more comprehensive analysis. Coleridge, whose genius combined in rarest union the emotional and imaginative nature of a poet with deep and subtil intellectual power, who was besides a master in experience, and well aware of its supreme importance in philosophy, was nevertheless caught and carried along by the wave of German ontological speculation, then swelling onwards almost irresistibly; and the best results were lost, which otherwise might well have followed from that rare combination of endowments. "My head was with Spinoza," he records in his *Biographia*, "my heart with Paul and John." Thank God for those words, and others of similar import scattered here and there throughout his writings. They at least indicate the aim, by describing the chief difficulty, of philosophy; namely, to produce a system which, by satisfying the claims, shall reconcile the antagonism of head and heart.

The chaos which arose from this break in the tradition of English philosophy John Stuart Mill endeavoured to reduce to order, by returning to the old basis of experience. This is an honour which can never be denied him. Nor have his efforts in this direction been fruitless. They have had a great and lasting effect, the benefit of which we are now reaping, although they were not crowned with complete success. From him we have again learnt the necessity of cleaving to experience, and building only on that traditional basis. But much more than this may be said of the writer whom I have named next to the Mills in my list, I mean John Grote, the author of *Exploratio Philosophica*. In that work, which was published in 1865, a comprehensive survey is made of the whole field of philosophy, its divisions are mapped afresh, the results of former progress are appraised and brought to a head, a new start is made on that basis, and a new, which is the present, epoch of English experiential philosophy begins. Due honour has never yet been done, in my opinion, to this great leader of philosophical thought, whose eminence time alone will fully bring to light. I think the writers whom I have named as belonging to one tradition, though I do not by any means put the list forward as exhaustive, may fairly be taken as representative of an English School, the characteristic mark of which may be called Experientialism, the resolve to obtain experience pure and simple, to see it whole and without addition, unmixed with imaginations, which come indeed from experience ultimately, but which have undergone modifications by filtration through the mental medium of the observer.*

Experientialism in this sense is not to be confounded with Positivism. Indeed Positivism supplies an instructive contrast. It simulates experientialism so far as its rejection of imagination goes, but it refuses to go all the way with experience. It begins by saying what kind of results it will aim at, what kind of enquiries it will alone consider valuable. It is as much an arbitrary dealing with experience by way of restriction, as overhaste to account for things by imagined entities or powers is an arbitrary dealing with it by way of amplification. We want the whole of experience on the one hand, as much as we want nothing but experience on the other. When once it is seen how difficult it is to obtain this, and that the source of the difficulty lies in the unconscious modifications of the human mind, arising partly from the mere process of association, partly from the interest with which we look on some things in preference to others, then we are led to devise methods for the express purpose of obtaining experiential data pure; and the name of an experiential method may fairly be given to any method devised for this purpose.—Be it noted, that I state the contrast between experience pure and experience adulterated in terms of ordinary life, and on the ordinary psychological assumption of minds in presence of an

* There is one writer in particular, the late Dean Mansel, whom I would gladly claim as a member of the English school, did the avowedly Kantian basis of his speculation permit. His refusal to follow Kant in that development of his theory which is contained in the *Critic of Practical Reason* is not the same thing as exchanging a Kantian for an experiential basis. Nevertheless it may be truly said, that, so far as the question of man's ability or inability to comprehend the Infinite is concerned, there are few to whom philosophy in this country owes a deeper debt, than to the brilliant author of the Bampton Lectures for 1858, on *The Limits of Religious Thought*.

external world. To state it in terms of philosophical analysis would be premature, even if it were possible; and moreover would not serve our present purpose of connecting philosophical with ordinary method.

Method in philosophy holds very much the same place that Hypothesis holds in science. Both must be tested by their results. But while results in science are tested by successful and verified prediction, and there is no prediction in philosophy, a Rationale of the Existent being its aim, the question is, what are the results which, in philosophy, test the value and soundness of the method? They are the removal of all gratuitous and merely logical puzzles, the harmonising of all parts or facts of consciousness, or what is the same thing, of experience, with each other, and thereby by degrees obtaining such a systematic Rationale of the whole, as was contemplated in my first Address, and there exhibited as the great purpose of philosophy. Puzzles are introduced into philosophy by making tacit and unsuspected assumptions; in contrast thereby to the assumptions of science, which are hypotheses adopted for some express purpose, and with full awareness of their hypothetical character. The soundness of a method in philosophy consists, therefore, in its leading to the successful detection and avoidance of unwitting assumptions.

Philosophy begins with questioning experience as it is found in the *præjudicia* of common sense, the world of common-sense things and persons, events and actions. The problems which it has to solve are proposed to it by the common-sense view of things; it does not invent, or begin by proposing, problems of its own. In growing up from infancy, we acquire a considerable measure of common-sense ideas and knowledge, habits and maxims, long before we philosophise, if indeed we ever arrive at philosophising at all. In those early years we are said to be acquiring experience, which is undeniably real, and often extremely definite, and extremely varied. We are moreover trained necessarily, from infancy, by the care of those about us, to think of objects, and to distinguish objects, in the way in which those about us have distinguished and thought about them. We grow up continuing and confirming the tradition of our elders. We group the same percepts together, and call them by the same names. Our native language becomes for us a familiar possession, corresponding in all its vocabulary, grammar, and idiom, to the supposed realities of things. Very high degrees of enlightenment, acuteness, culture, and refinement, may be, and often are, reached by persons who have never made any scientific or technical acquisition, outside this ordinary circle of ideas, which is common to the scientific and the unscientific alike, the ordinary world of common sense.

It must not be supposed, that this common-sense world, this common-sense way of viewing experience, is ever reversed or abolished, or imagined by philosophers to be so, in favour of some other more accurate results of science or of philosophy, which step into its place. When this idea is entertained, it is due to a prejudice of common sense itself. Scientific or philosophic results, compared to the ideas of common sense, are not opposed to them as the *real* is opposed to the *apparent*. The difference is not in point of reality, but in point of method, and strictness in obeying it. Standing on the level of common-sense knowledge, as his acknowledged basis and starting-point, the man of science proceeds to analyse, to compare, to measure, to make experiments, to frame hypotheses, to predict, to verify. In all this, he never leaves the order of ideas which we designate common sense. His molecules and atoms are but ordinary visible and tangible bodies, taken on a smaller scale, and with their actions imagined as corresponding to their number, size, position, and environment, precisely as if they were ordinary bodies in ordinary environments.

What science does is simply to apply a mental microscope, telescope, and magnifying glass, to the ordinary world, thereby revealing in detail, and summing up in general and abstract statements, the hidden mechanism by which it works. Mathematic in its two branches of geometry and calculation, combined with experiment in actual matter,—this is the great instrument of the revelation. Another world, and yet the same, is thus created, as it were, from the ribs of the old world of common sense. Eve is evoked from Adam's side. Familiarity is the note of the old world, law of the new. The same phenomena are distributed afresh. Instead of being seen in result, they are seen in process of production and operation. But every class of contributories to the result is separately examined, and falls under a special branch of science. And this separate examination it is, which enables the process of production and operation to be seen; enables the mental construction of the whole, by showing how the several kinds of matter and energy, which have been severally studied by the several sciences, are actually combined.

Two ways of examining experience and acquiring fresh knowledge from the examination are now in outline before us; the first is that of common sense, which gives us our ordinary and familiar world; the second is that of science, which traces the laws and mechanism of that same world, mechanism and laws which, but for what I have called the mental lens of science, would have been totally hidden from us. But as it is, there is no corner of the world into which it does not pry, in search for the causes of things. Consider but the array presented by the greater divisions of the army of those sciences which, from the perfect generality of their scope, may be called speculative. At the head of all stand the mathematical sciences, calculation, geometry, kinematic. Next come those which treat of force as manifested in inorganic matter, dynamics and statics; then chemistry; then those parts of physics which have what are called the imponderables for their object; then, passing to organic matter, biology; and lastly that science, to which it belongs to examine the deepest forces which are operative in human consciousness, psychology.

Add to these the divisions of the other wing of the scientific army, I mean the chronological and historical wing, relating to the actual series of events which we have reason to think has taken place, and is taking place, in our world,—astronomy, geology, botany, zoology, comprising the theory of the evolution of living beings, as well as that of the social and political evolution of the educable races, mankind at the head of them.

Lastly consider the list of what, in comparison with what I have called the speculative and the historical, may best perhaps be called the practical group of sciences, I mean those under which are ranged, and by means of which are deduced, the various arts of life, from the mechanical arts at one end of the series to the *ars artium* at the other, the art of living well, both for individuals and for communities,—ethic, politic, and also, in view of man's connection with the Universe, as well as with the earth and the inhabitants of earth, theology, the study of man's relations with the Divine.

Science and common sense, the world as known by science, and the world as known by common sense, two faculties and two worlds, the same and yet different, which might seem not only mutually to supplement one another, as in fact they do, but also to exhaust between them all possible fields and kinds of knowledge, so that what was not within possible contemplation as a problem for science could not possibly arise as a problem at all. Common sense at the periphery, and science at the centre, seem to have the whole sphere of existence within their range, at any rate, though they may not be able to penetrate every recess therein. But the point to which I wish to lead you is, that this is not entirely so; that there is an omission on the part of both the faculties or methods now named, which is fatal to their claim of all-comprehensiveness; that there is a third faculty or method, which rectifies that omission, seizes on a question which has been passed over, and thereby educes a third world, a world again different and yet again the same, from the ribs of the second, as the second was educed from the ribs of the first;—and that this third faculty is philosophy.

Familiarity, I said above, is the note of the common-sense world; common sense takes its objects as given, as ready-made and given objects; asking no question as to what *giving* is, that is, what it is to *exist* and *be*. In this point, science exactly follows her lead; she changes indeed the *personnel*, so to speak, of the existents; she speaks of molecules, atoms, ethers, motions, and so on, as existent, where common sense spoke of rocks and trees, light and air, plants and animals, as existent; but the conception of *existence* is left where it was, unquestioned. The supposed Cosmic Nebula, when it is supposed, is supposed to have existed, is taken as an existent. But what is an existent? What is it to *Be?* What do we mean by *Being?*

The question in this wide generality of meaning, for there is nothing to which it does not apply, is never asked either by common sense or by science. Existence is taken as something *per se notum*. In other words, existents, τὰ ὄντα, are taken as *absolutes*, independent of anything else, unless it be other existents, fragments as it were of causal energy striking root of themselves, though derived originally, it may be, from some primeval but existent source, underived itself, the *Causa Sui et Mundi.* Such is the problem transmitted by common sense and science to philosophy,—the problem of the absolute,— What is it to *Be?*

Now this question opens an entirely new domain, an entirely new series, of enquiries. The question, not the answer to it, is the entrance to philosophy. It is not as if philosophy had a new and striking answer to give to this question at first setting out, an answer which, carrying conviction with it, thereby proved the value of philosophy, by helping science and common sense out of an embarrassment. The answer ultimately given by philosophy is one implicitly known already, and even when given produces no impression of novelty. It is the question which is important, as being the first of a new kind of questions, a kind which puts a new face upon the whole of knowledge, and evokes a third out of the two former worlds, different from and yet the same with them both.

The question about *Being* is a limit-question; the whole of experience is included in it. We cannot go beyond experience, and assign a larger term, under which Being can be subsumed, and so explained. It may be pictured either as lying within a fixed barrier set to thought, with vacuity, that is, non-being, beyond it, or as lying within an elastic barrier to thought, which recedes as thought advances, so as to include every new object thought of. It is one of those ultimate terms, to seek a reason for which is to destroy reason, in Aristotle's phrase. In all rational account of anything, Being must be taken as known, in order to obtain a rational account at all. When therefore we reach this limit, when we ask the question, What *Being* means?—then it is plain we in some sort turn back upon our own footsteps; we no longer go on to a further explanation, beyond Being, but we ask this question in a different sense from the previous ones. In what sense do we ask it? Clearly in the sense of bringing to light some thought, or some feature, which was implicitly present in our use of the term, but which we have not had explicitly presented to us. What is that *we mean* by this term *Being*, which we have been using? Such is our question. And this question is plainly reflective or retrospective, and aims at obtaining a further and more distinct knowledge of our own knowing.

Yet note, on the other hand, that the question does not relate solely to our own individual knowledge, or to ourselves, as something different and apart from the things to which we apply the term *being*. If that were the case, the question would be already classed as belonging to psychology, from its assuming the existence of Subjects; and at the same time would be guilty of the absurdity of assuming its own answer to be already known, inasmuch as both we and our knowledge would be assumed as really existing, that is, as belonging to an already known category. But this is not the sense or scope of the question about the meaning of the term *being* generally. The question is, not how we, as individual beings, come to use this term in preference to other terms, but what relation between knowledge and objects of knowledge is designated by it. Not the relation between one class of objects and another, not the relation either between things and things, or between thoughts and thoughts, but the relation between things generally and thoughts generally, or between objects and knowledge of them, is the thing aimed at.

This circumstance, this drift of the question, it is, which gives it cardinal importance in opening up the philosophical line of enquiry, as distinguished from the common-sense and the scientific lines. The relation be-

B

tween thoughts and things, between objective thought and objects thought of, between knowledge and reality, or in one word, between the subjective and objective aspects of existence,—this is the peculiar aim and province of philosophy, as distinguished from the two other lines of thought which precede it. The field is the same, but in philosophy it is considered always in a double reference, or under a double aspect. Knowledge and its object, not the knowing being and the things he knows, —this is the distinction in which philosophy originates, and by which it is governed. This distinction also gives it greater grasp. For the knowing being cannot otherwise be got at. He is an object thought of; to assume *him* as the subjective aspect of the remainder of the universe is to assume one atom of the universe as the subjective equivalent of the whole, and that without throwing any new light on his own nature. He, as a real existent and agent, endowed with real powers and modes of feeling, knowing, and acting, is the object of psychology. His knowledge, abstracting from the laws of that agency by which in him it is brought about,—his knowledge, compared not with its real conditions in him, but with the real objects of which it is the knowledge,— and having those real objects confronted with it,—that is to say, the relation between knowing, as such, and being, as such,—this is the first starting-point and standing ground of philosophy, in the strict sense of the term.

Philosophy is thus as properly a theory of knowing as of being, as much an enquiry into the nature of knowledge as into the nature of existence. It is the one just because it is the other. The two aspects are inseparable. Knowledge is the subjective aspect of existence, and existence the objective aspect of knowledge. This is sometimes expressed by saying, that we know something *of* something else. It is this relation to its own subjective aspect, to knowledge generally, that is meant by the phrase *relativity of existence;* not its relation to *us* as the Subjects of the knowledge. Any relation of an existent to us, as Subjects of the knowledge of it, would be a relation of it to other existents, a relation not between knowing and being, but between two or more beings, two or more existents. It is knowledge, not man, that is the subjective aspect of existence; not man, but man's knowledge that in a certain sense, is πάντων μέτρον. Thus not only does the relativity or doubleness of aspect exclude the idea of absolute existence, but the exclusion of it is owing to something which is at once essential to knowledge, namely, its being necessarily knowledge *of* something, and at the same time essential to existence, namely, its being necessarily existence for knowledge, since otherwise the term *existence* would be meaningless. It is in this sense, and for this reason only, that the Absolute is an impossible and self-contradictory idea. So far from the Absolute being, as sometimes supposed, the object-matter which is characteristic of philosophy, the reverse is the case. It is rather a conception characteristic of common sense and positive science, in contradistinction from philosophy. From these philosophy inherits it, as a conception till then undoubted, a conception the legitimacy of which it alone is in a position to criticise. Absolutes are physical, not metaphysical, entities; the Absolute is a scientific, not a philosophical, conception.

I hope I have now made it evident, that philosophy is no pursuit apart from the interests and methods of ordinary life, requiring some special intuition, or based on some special axioms, which men in general cannot be expected to admit; but that it is the third and last of a group or series of methods, which together cover the whole field of knowledge real or possible, the two prior members of which are common sense and positive science.

Moreover it will be evident, I hope, that it is in a most important sense continuous with these prior methods, springing out of them simply by turning their object-matter round, as it were, and bringing another aspect of it into view, taking their largest and limiting category, that of *Being*, and instituting a retrospective and critical enquiry into it as such, that is, in its character of the largest and limiting category of experience.

But what is the enabling principle, I would ask in the next place, or rather what principle of method is necessarily involved in our thus taking the category of Being in this its utmost and all-embracing scope? We are enabled to do so simply in virtue of our distinguishing and abstracting from the question *how comes*, and retaining solely the question *what is*. How *Being* comes to *be* Being,—this is plainly a question which cannot be propounded without contradiction in the thought of the propounder. *Being* in its largest scope plainly includes the Being of causes as well as the Being of effects. And therefore to ask how Being comes to Be is either self-contradictory, or else asked about Being in the sense of conditioned Being only, and not of Being conditioned and unconditioned alike, nor yet of Being conditioning only. The question, *what Being is*, is prior to every other in a comprehensive, critical, and retrospective enquiry. Causation or Conditioning is a distinction which pre-supposes Being generally. And the question, when taken in this large sense, can mean only, What is meant by Being, or in other words, What is its subjective aspect, its *differentia* in knowledge?

In short, there is but one way of approaching the question of Being, which is the question of philosophy. It consists in asking what we know of it, what Being is *known as?* In this consists the constantly remarked *subjective* character of modern philosophy. Aristotle's First

Philosophy, or Theology, afterwards called **Metaphysic**, marked out for itself the enquiry into Being as its field,— τὸ ὂν ᾗ ὄν, καὶ τὰ τούτῳ ὑπάρχοντα καθ' αὑτό. The progress of modern times has slowly brought us to see, that the only way of enquiring into Being is to enquire what we *know* of Being, or what Being is *known as*. With this change to subjectivity in the method, Aristotle's view of the scope of philosophy remains true. It is still *Being* that is the object of it, only that we are now aware of the fact, that we see it, not from outside, but from within, the philosopher being himself taken as a part of the whole object contemplated; or, to put the same thing in another way, abstraction being made of who or where is the contemplator, and attention being fixed solely on the content contemplated.

When the Absolute is taken as the object, or part of the object, of philosophy, a wider field is apparently taken, but a narrower one really. It is sometimes said, that all knowledge is indeed of the relative, but that this relative knowledge of ours necessarily implies an absolute and unknowable reality beyond our knowledge. The Absolute is thus made to appear as an unknowable, self-existent, background to knowledge. But again the question occurs,—is not this very statement of the Absolute a statement of it as relative? It would seem that, granting we cannot grasp the Absolute, we can and do grasp our knowledge of it, so that the question of its *Being* becomes again the question, What its Being is *known as*?

Or again another turn may be given to the thought of the Absolute, by regarding it as containing either the conditions of the relative, or the conditions of our knowledge of the relative. The Absolute then becomes the Transcendent, or the Noumenal, as opposed to the phenomenal in knowledge, or the phenomenal in existence.

But again the same remark is applicable. The terms *transcendent* and *noumenal* are only apparently wider and larger than the term *phenomenal*. They are so apparently, because they cover a region of conditions, which is indefinite compared to the conditioned existence, and conditioned knowledge, with which they are contrasted. They are not so really, because, granting the real conditions of that indefinite region, still we surmise them as part of Being, and after all it is but the content of one part of our knowledge, namely, our surmise, which is larger than that of another part, namely, our more definite knowledge. In short, the distinctions between the Absolute and the Relative, the Transcendent and the Phenomenal, the Noumenal and the Phenomenal, are as much distinctions in the content of our knowledge, as they are in the content of Being, the object of knowledge.

Similar remarks apply to another conception which is a derivative of two of the foregoing, the transcendent and the noumenal. I mean the conception of *a priori* Forms, in which all phenomenal knowledge, and consequently all phenomena which are its objects, are restricted to appear. By their aid the noumenal and transcendent Subject is supposed to carve, or construct, out of the noumenal and transcendent Object, the phenomenally objective world. The *a priori* Forms mediate, as it were, between the two otherwise unknowable regions of existence, and render the Absolute phenomenally manifest. But the transcendent Subject and the transcendent Object are entirely hypothetical. Since they are assumed as ir themselves unknowable, it is a pure hypothesis to assig them the functions indicated by the names Subject ar Object. That the Forms, called *a priori*, are consta and, so far as we can see, essential features, in phenome and phenomenal knowledge or experience, is no grou for supposing that they have a root or source in someth which on the one hand exists, but on the other cannot be thought of, independently of themselves. Moreover, granting that they had a source in the unknowable and the absolute, still they would help us only to a partial and incidental view of that world which they are supposed to manifest; the phenomenal world would be merely the world as seen by those beings, in whose constitution these particular *a priori* Forms were inwrought, or on whose cognitive powers they were imposed.

The Kantian Transcendental Hypothesis, therefore,—for you will have seen that this is what is in question,—so far from bearing a philosophical character, so far from affording a free and unrestricted outlook over the whole field of knowledge, existence, or experience, bears a character the very opposite, the character, I mean, of a scientific hypothesis, an hypothesis to account for the genesis of human experience as we know it, on the assumption that it is *not* experience of the truth of things. Four assumptions are made,—first that there is an unknowable Absolute, next that there are transcendent Agencies therein, thirdly that these agencies act in certain known Forms, and lastly that these actions constitute human experience. By these assumptions it is sought to connect human experience with the unknowable source and centre of absolute existence.

Philosophy, however, painfully aware of long and fruitless wanderings in these quasi-scientific and non-philosophic paths, has come at last to put the simple question—What is there in experience to justify the assumption of an Unknowable Absolute at all? She recalls the circumstance, that, in every moment or instance of distinct knowing, that is, of consciousness, the distinction of *knowing* from *being known* is observable, and suspects that the *being known* has been erected into an unknowable existence by an illusory separation from its other aspect or moment, *knowing*, which is really in expe rience inseparable from it; arguing that, if experience i the test of truth, an unknowable existence is a fiction Farther she reminds us, that the business of experience which is also the business of philosophy, is not to *be*, bu to *know;* and that, since, in knowing, the known i always involved, and we never know without knowin; something, therefore we cannot in experience, or i philosophy, escape from the inseparability of the tw moments.

Supposing, indeed, it were our business, in philosophy not to know but to *be*, then indeed it might for a instant be imagined, that we could very well *be* withou knowing it, and thus that the moment of *being* was sepai able. But would our *being*, even then, be wholly un known,—unknown to intelligence in every respect, a (by supposition) to ourselves? Surely not. We canno make the supposition, that our own being is unknown t intelligence in every respect, and therefore it is a verbe fallacy to profess to do so, for we are assuming it a known, namely, to ourselves now, in making the suppc sition itself. It is only to ourselves in a restricted sense namely, as particular objects of our present knowledge that we can suppose our own being to be unknown. being wholly and in every respect unknown is a *not-being* In the very meaning of *being*, knowability is involvec To escape, therefore, from the ultimate inseparability c the two moments of experience, knowing and bein, known, is to escape not from relative into absolute exist ence, but from relative existence into nonentity. B Being, by Existence, we mean that which is of a piec with what is known, and not that which is known a unknowable, or which is unrelated in relation to know ledge. The conception which, on the experiential metho of philosophy, replaces that of the unknowable absolut is the conception of the Universe, regarded in its deepest, essential, and constant features.

At the same time it must be distinctly remarked, that, while the very nature of knowledge excludes the existence of an *unknowable*, this same nature of knowledge involves, and necessarily involves, the existence of an *unknown*. Knowledge has been described above as being always knowledge *of* something, we know something of something else. The *something* is the known part, and the *something else* is the unknown part of our knowledge. The *something* is "objective thought," and the *something else* is "object thought of,"—expressions which will be familiar to you from my last Address. Our knowledge is thus, as it were, at every moment *astride* the universe of things, one side known, the other unknown. Of the unknown side we know two things, first that it is unknown, and secondly that it is the other side of, and continuous with, the known. It is no unknowable, transcendent, noumenal, or absolute existence, but a constant category in our knowledge, applicable now to one thing, now to another, owing to the fact, that knowing is a process. Just as light reveals three things, itself, and objects, and darkness, so knowledge reveals itself, the known, and the unknown. The darkness is as much a phenomenon to light, as the light itself and the illumined objects are; and similarly the unknown is a phenomenon to knowledge, just as rightfully as the knowledge itself and the objects known. The unknown is no unknowable existent, but a category, and constant as a category, in our knowledge.

It is evident, moreover, that we can ascribe no really effective content or character to the unknown, except by ascribing to it characteristics drawn from our knowledge of the known, and imagining it to act in ways analogous to those of known real agents. Theories, therefore, which hypostasise the unknown as a noumenal or transcendent agent, or agents, are really making hypotheses similar to the hypotheses of positive science, in a field which avowedly lies beyond the reach, not of positive science only, but of every kind of speculative knowledge. What justification can there be for ascribing agency at all, or any other attribute which draws its meaning from experience, to the absolutely unknowable? It is ascribing efficient agency to nothingness. If however, as philosophy must maintain, our knowledge of the unknown is derived from that of the known, as the knowledge of darkness is derived from that of light, then, and from this point of view, which is the subjective point of view of philosophy, we embrace even the unknown in our purview, when we put the first question of philosophy,— What *Being* means. We embrace the unknown as a category or rubric including unknown objects, but without hypostasising it as an absolute First Cause.

Slightly to vary the expression of my meaning, the conception of Things-in-themselves, or unknowable existents, and the distinction between them and phenomena, are a part of our way of regarding experience, and ought therefore to be reckoned to method, and not made absolute. Making the distinction absolute is a remnant of the objective method in philosophy, surviving even in Kantianism. The distinction by which it is replaced, on the subjective and experiential method, is that between things regarded in their *thatness*, or as *de facto* existents, and the same things regarded in their *whatness*, or as known in consciousness. The old distinction is given up, not so much because the conception on which it rests (existents known to be unknowable) is self-contradictory, as because it is an assumption made concerning the universe, prior to examining our knowledge of the universe. The mystery of *de facto* existence may remain for ever as unfathomable by the subjective method, as it is represented to be by the old distinction. But it will not also, and at the same time, be represented as a mystery attaching to a definite object, or objects, isolated from knowledge,—which is the conception required by the old distinction,—instead of attaching to *de facto* existence altogether.

It is cheering to see, that even Germans are at last awaking to a partial sense of these truths, are becoming alive to the untenability both of Kant's Transcendentalism, and of the subjective or idealistic Absolutism which was its natural development, are beginning to conceive subjective analysis of experience as the main business of philosophy, and philosophy itself as a work to which all genuine students may contribute something, instead of being the appanage of some individual genius who, reading by inspiration the riddle of the universe, and giving a name to the energy known, by an *a priori* assumption, to be its eternal source, may construct once and for all the sole sufficient theory of its system. I refer more particularly to a recent work, in which these views are expressed, Dr. R. von Schubert-Soldern's *Grundlagen einer Erkenntnisstheorie,* Leipzig, 1884, in the Introduction to which (p. 3) the names of several other well-known writers are mentioned, as representatives, in different degrees, of the same general line of thought.

Cheering, however, as it doubtless is, to find that views, which harmonise so well with what one has been maintaining for twenty years, are at last beginning to recommend themselves to notice, yet an Englishman may well be permitted to doubt, whether a method, which has the appearance of being simply a revival of Kantianism *minus* Kant's transcendental hypotheses, can either itself take the place of philosophy, or be of any real service as its preliminary or propædeutic. In fact we are compelled to put the question to this new creation of the German mind, *Erkenntnisstheorie*, which seems to have taken the place of Ontology deceased, on what ground it professes to stand. Does it stand on the ground of common sense, or of psychology, or of philosophy? Or is it merely a new *a priori* logic of abstractions?

Kant's critical and transcendental system, which is contained in his three great works, the *Critic of Pure Reason*, the *Critic of Practical Reason*, and the *Critic of Judgment*, was in reality a piece of psychology founded on unwarranted and even unthinkable assumptions. He himself regarded it merely as the preliminary to a philosophy, or philosophical Doctrine, which should consist of two branches, one theoretical, the other practical, one being the *Metaphysic of Nature*, the other the *Metaphysic of Morals*. This conception of philosophy as a doctrine of reality, having two branches theoretical (or speculative as I prefer to call it) and practical, was no doubt perfectly correct in itself, and so far as it went, being founded on facts of immediate experience. Kant was only wrong in allowing it to be overridden by the psychological conception of a "pure" knowledge derived from *a priori* principles; the carrying out of which latter conception could issue only in systems of Idealistic Ontology, which was in fact the result in Germany. It is true, that these systems made away, more or less completely, with Kant's idea of *Things-in-themselves;* but this is only one part, and that the dependent part, of his whole hypothesis. They still retained the hypothesis of energy, or agency, somewhere or somehow bound up with consciousness, or with the Subject as distinguished from Objects, and therefore still attempted to construct their objective world *a priori*.

Kant's view of philosophy as a doctrine of reality, having two branches, theoretical (or speculative) and practical, the general truth of which is verified by experience, is what we, at the present day, have still to work out; not however on *a priori* principles, but by subjective analysis of experience, independent of psychological assumptions. But what is meant by a Theory of Knowledge? Kant's position at any rate was perfectly intelligible. His hypothesis of a noumenal Subject, endowed with definite faculties, each of which worked in distinct and nameable forms, supplied him with a basis, on which his criticism of knowledge and its necessary limits could be founded. And such a criticism could plausibly lay claim to be a necessary preliminary for a positive doctrine of Being. But a system of general criticism of knowledge does not become philosophy, merely by omitting psychological assumptions. What vantage-ground does the knowledge criticising occupy, in respect of the knowledge criticised? On what basis does its criticism rest? It has the appearance of being psychology omitting the psychical agent, instead of imagining a fictitious one, as Kant did. But to surrender one basis is not to acquire another. Its being bad as psychology does not show, that it is good as philosophy. Philosophy has aims and requirements of its own, to which a mere Theory of Knowledge is presumably inadequate. On the one hand, philosophy is the theory of Being; not of knowledge only (*Erkenntnisstheorie*), but of Knowing and Being together. And on the other hand, to say that a method is analysis, or even subjective analysis, is not to show its sufficiency as a method. Not analysis only, but a method of the analysis, a guide in analysing, is required; a guide, however, which at the same time shall not import any foregone conclusion, or pre-conceived ideas, into the analytic process or its results. This guide, as you will remember, I suppose myself to have found in "the distinction between conditions of essence and conditions of existence." And some such guide at any rate seems necessary, before we can speak of subjective analysis as a sufficient and independent method of philosophising.

For these reasons, while adopting subjective analysis as the main and fundamental business of philosophy, and standing thus on the traditional ground of the English school, a frank appeal to experience and experience alone, I also characterise philosophy by its traditional name of *Metaphysic*, indicating thereby, that it is no mere preliminary criticism of the cognitive powers, no mere proprædeutic of investigations into the laws of Being, but that it is at one and the same time a critical investigation into what we know, and an analytical investigation into what we know as being. The name *Theory of Knowledge* (*Erkenntnisstheorie*), which is also, I believe, derived originally from Kant, is open, in my opinion, to precisely the same objection in principle, as the opposite name *Ontology* would be, if applied to philosophy. The one suggests that Knowledge can be studied apart from Being; the other, that Being can be studied apart from Knowledge, and thus that the absolute essence of the universe can be grasped by man, revealed by some *a priori* intuition superior to criticism.

Again, a Theory of Knowledge, which is not also at the same time a Theory of Being, is but a particular or special branch of knowledge, founded on the fact, that its object, knowledge, has been marked off from other objects, previous to being made the object of a theory. Standing thus on a prior distinction, which it adopts ready drawn to its hand from elsewhere, a Theory of Knowledge which is not also a Theory of Being is dependent on that prior distribution of object-matter which it adopts, and therefore on some Theory of Being prior to itself. Dependence and speciality, therefore, are suggested by the very name *Theory of Knowledge*, and render it unsuitable to be the name of an enquiry, which lays claim, as philosophy, to complete autonomy and perfect comprehensiveness.]

II.

TURNING, then, from this view of philosophy which I have now taken, as the last in a series of three modes of regarding things, the two first being common sense and positive science, I come to a closer consideration of its method, or mode of operation in articulating a system of philosophical thought, including the general heads of division and distribution of the object-matter, which arise in consequence of the guiding distinction of its method being applied thereto. And in the first place I would note, that this guiding distinction, by which of course I mean the distinction between conditions of essence and conditions of existence, or nature and genesis, is not invented or arbitrarily adopted by philosophy, but that it is found already implicit in every, even the simplest, act of questioning, or attention to a content; and that this universality of its presence in all questioning is one necessary condition of its validity, when chosen as the guiding distinction of philosophy, that is, when explicitly adopted as the guide in putting the first strictly philosophical question, the limit-question, *What is Being?* and the further questions which result from the answer first obtained to it.

For philosophy at starting does not begin with a *tabula rasa*, but with a known and familiar world of objects already given; that is to say, it begins from the ordinary world of common sense, the world of empirical *absolutes*, things and persons, events and actions. No one begins to philosophise at birth. It is only about the common-sense world and its objects that the philosophic question *What?* can originally be put. A man who begins to philosophise is already familiar with this world, and with himself as an inhabitant and member of it. In most cases also he is familiar with some parts of the world of positive science, which is also a world of absolutes, though consisting of a different set from those of the common-sense world. By *himself*, for instance, he means, in common sense, his consciousness and his organism together; in the science of psychology, he means by it the real agent animating his organism, whatever that agent may turn out to be. These two worlds being presupposed, philosophy begins with the simple question— What is meant by the *Being* of them?—expecting an answer different in kind from the answers given by common sense and positive science, inasmuch as the question has a different sense, namely this,—How is *Being* to be characterised, seeing that there is no larger category, as there is in the case of everything else, under which it can be subsumed, and from which it can be distinguished by differentiation, and in that manner classified?

Observe another point also. A conscious being and its consciousness, belonging originally to the world of common sense and science, now come to belong, in asking this question, to the world of philosophy. That is to say, not the Object of knowledge only, but the Subject of it also passes over into the philosophic domain, with the putting of this limit-question. The same consciousness is continued into a new line of enquiry. The consciousness is continued; the new departure being marked only by a particular kind of question being asked, the limit-question about *Being*. Philosophic consciousness is thus a continuation of pre-philosophic; that is to say, it is a continuation of that consciousness which has developed with our development from infancy onwards, and as part of which our whole knowledge of the objects composing the common sense and scientific worlds has developed up to the point marked by the first philosophic or limit-question.

Observe also, that the objects of the pre-philosophic world consist really of objective and subjective aspects together, just as much as those of the philosophic world do, though it is not consciously and explicitly observed that they do so, prior to the philosophic question. Indeed this is the very fact which becomes explicit in the first answer to the limit-question, *What is Being?* that answer consisting in this, as I have brought out in a former Address, that *esse* is *percipi;* which is simply assigning an obverse aspect to *being,* namely *knowing,* and at the same time an obverse aspect to *knowing,* namely *being.*

Philosophic consciousness, then, is a continuation of that pre-philosophic consciousness which has developed with us from infancy onwards, and which has given us our knowledge of the empirical objects of common sense and science. And it is also essential to notice, that this last named knowledge has been attained by the very same method of questioning and attention which is continued into philosophy, I mean by asking the question *what,* as the prior indispensable condition of asking the further question *how comes,* in any and every object. The question *what* is the name or formula describing the purpose of the act of attention as a cognitive or perceptive act. And obviously, to have a content distinctly present to consciousness, which is the purpose of this act, and which is expressed by the question, *what is this content,* is a pre-requisite to asking distinctly any other question about it, such as, what it resembles, or from what it differs, or generally in what relations it stands to other contents or objects of consciousness, among which relations is the relation to its conditions of existence, or things to which it stands related as a dependent. Observe, I speak only of distinct perceptions. I do not deny, that difference indistinctly perceived is a pre-requisite of distinct perception. But I maintain, that a distinct perception of what a percept is *per se*, or in relation to consciousness alone, is both logically and psychologically a pre-requisite to its being compared with other percepts, and consequently prior to classifying and naming it.

One more point remains to be noted in regard to the continuation of pre-philosophic consciousness into philosophic. It is this. Putting the limit-question about Being, which marks the transition, is not putting a question about the nature of the knowing agent, or Subject, as distinguished from the nature of the things known, or Object. It is one thing to ask a question about the nature of Being generally, under which both the Subject and the Object are included, and quite another thing to ask a question about the differentia of the Subject from the Object. The distinction between these two questions lies across the threshold of philosophy, and confusing them prevents numbers from ever setting foot within philosophy at all.*

The confusion is increased and worse confounded by the circumstance, that the most usual and almost necessary phrases by which knowledge is described, those for instance which employ "I" and "We" and their derivatives, afford no aids to perceiving the distinction, but rather help to obliterate and obscure it. For it always seems, in consequence of their use, that a question about *our* knowledge, *we* being the Subjects knowing, must be a question about *ourselves*, and that a question about the *objects* of our knowledge must be a question about the objects as distinguished from the part which *we* contribute to the knowledge of them. Besides which, very many of the important substantive words in constant use are ambiguous, from including more than one distinguishable thing in their meaning. *Perception* and

* On this point see my paper, *Subjectivity in Philosophy,—A Reply* in MIND, xxix. Jan. 1883.

knowing, for instance, even after being distinguished from *percept* and *thing known*, imply an action, as well as a state, or a content, of consciousness. The structure of language may indeed afford many useful hints as to the mechanism of thought, but it is very far from being an adequate mirror of its subtilties.

Now the truth is that, in putting the limit-question, *What is Being?*—our Self, or Subject, or knowing Agent, is properly included among the Beings concerning whom (or which) that question is asked; and when we put that question under the guidance of our method, we consciously and purposely include it among them. In putting it, therefore, we consciously abstract from the circumstance, that a Subject is required to put it, and is putting it actually; and we leave the special nature of that Subject, which for our thought at the time is an existent Object, for future enquiry, along with other Objects, when once we shall have seen what is the nature of Being, the nature which is shared by all Objects alike. The question concerning the nature of Being concerns all Existents alike, including consciousness itself when taken as an existent; all alike, including consciousness itself, being distinguished from the nature of Knowledge, taken as knowledge.

But why and how, it may be asked, is the Subject for us an existent Object, when its very name indicates its essential contrast with objects, and when without it all knowledge, the whole subjective aspect of things, would confessedly be impossible? The answer is plain from what has gone before. The Subject is to us, when entering on philosophy, an object among objects, because we then have before us, no *tabula rasa*, but the world of empirical objects as known to common sense and positive science. If philosophy were an *a priori* construction out of intuitions, or laws of thought, independent of the empirical world, the case would be altered. We should

then have no other source to go to, for the fundamenta
intuitions or laws of our construction, but some hypo
thesis or other concerning the nature of abstract intelli
gence hypostasised as an agent. But as it is, we have
a familiar knowledge of ourselves as empirical existents
to begin with and to question, just as much as we have
of empirical existents which are not ourselves. Just as
much knowledge, and it must be added, just as little
However certain we may be of the independent agency o
material things, it is yet extremely improbable that we
possessed this idea, still more that we felt certain of its
truth, when, as newly born infants, we experienced visua
and tactual perceptions for the first time in combination
Similarly, however certain we may be of the independen
agency of our immaterial Self, it is equally improbable
that we possessed this idea, with certainty of its truth
in the first moments of conscious life or conscious per
ception. No. The existence of Matter and the existence
of Mind, as we think of them and believe in them when
we begin to philosophise, are equally familiar, equally
questionable, equally products of experience from infancy
onwards, equally formed out of perceptions by means o
inference and verification, equally therefore dependen
upon putting the questions *what* and *how comes*, which are
the very same questions by which they have again in
philosophy to be tested.

Here, then, we begin to see, and shall see still more
clearly as we advance, the drift and function of ou
guiding distinction of method, namely, that it raises
explicitly this very question, which lies across the thresh
old of philosophy, and forbids an answer to it being
given hastily, one way or the other, without a distinc
consciousness of the confusion to which it is exposed
The distinction is a necessary one in all questioning, a
we have already seen; that is, it is one which sooner

later must be brought to bear upon all parts, all views, of knowledge or reality; and therefore it cannot be pretended that, by putting it in this instance, we are rendering impossible beforehand the answer which I have now supposed may be due to confusion, the answer affirming the complete and ultimate coalescence of consciousness and the conscious agent, or Subject, into a single Existent.

We may conceivably find hereafter, that this coalescence is a necessary inference concerning the primary constitution of consciousness; and if so, since consciousness is confessedly in some sense co-extensive with existence, that is to say, no one (barring believers in the Unknowable, to whom all things are possible) can think of anything's existing without thinking in general terms of the thing itself, it would follow at once, that the existence of Subjects and their consciousness was the only existence possible, being that mode of it in which all other modes were included; and thereby the theory known as Idealism would be forthwith established. But plainly this answer, which affirms the necessary coalescence of consciousness and Subjects of consciousness into existent units, in the character of mutual contributories to, co-elements or co-factors of, each other's existence, and that of the unit they compose, cannot be admitted without first distinctly raising the questions,— what consciousness *per se* is known as, and what the Subject *per se* is known as, apart from the questions,—what consciousness as known, and what the Subject as known, respectively depend on, whether either of them is self-dependent, or *causa sui*, or whether they are mutually dependent on each other. By saying that every *being* has a *knowing* as its obverse aspect, it is not meant, that the being *knows*, or is the bearer of the knowledge in question, which would be predicating action of the being, but only that it *is known*, that *esse* is *percipi*. Whether it is also always and necessarily the bearer of the knowledge, or whether another being is sometimes or always requisite to know it,—these are points not pre-judged by the statement, but intended to be reserved for future enquiry.

A

Distinction of Aspects.

And now to summarise the results of the foregoing remarks, and report progress so far as we have gone. The simple fact of perception over against the simple fact of something perceived,—a doubleness of fact against fact which is itself perceived only in and by becoming afterwards a simple fact perceived, over against the simple perception of it, or which, in other words, is a fact repeated in all immediately observed instances of perception or thought, that is to say, in all remembered or renewable experience,—is that relation which we characterise as the relation of the subjective and objective aspects to each other. The psychological name for the secondary perceptual act, which is the act constitutive of experience, or in which experience is constantly originating, —and by psychological name I mean its name as a function among other functions of a conscious being,—which name also marks its character as perception, not simply of percepts, but of perception of percepts,—is *Reflection*, or in Kant's nomenclature *Apperception*. The perceptive act of one moment is objective to the perceptive act of the subsequent moment, and in that second act we perceive two things, 1st the content *of* consciousness, or whatness, of the first act, 2nd the fact that it was perceived, and has now become a content *for* consciousness.

But a name will also be required for those perceptive acts, which *per se*, or until perceived by subsequent acts, are not conscious perceptions of aspects, but simply acts of, or states or events in, consciousness. These may perhaps be best called *primary perceptions*, or states of primary consciousness, and their content *primary percepts*. But we must remember that the same doubleness of aspect is really involved in them, only that we do not distinctly perceive it without an act of attention, the supervening of which is the arising of a secondary perception, or reflection. I mean, that even in primary perceptions we must distinguish, in thought, the process of perception, as an act or event, and the completion of it as a state or content, in consciousness; that is, distinguish the *perceiving* from the *percept;* without considering them as objective to consciousness, until the secondary act supervenes.

These, then, are the two aspects. Both are objective to the secondly perceptive, or reflective, act; that is, are for it existents; and also, from being inseparable in perception, are obverse aspects of existence. Whatever we in any way perceive, have cognisance of, or imagine,— that we say *exists*. If the term *existence* has meaning at all, it must at the least have this meaning. And this relation we can, in thought, distinguish from all others, irrespective of whether or not we may afterwards find, that the two aspects have necessarily any other relations, besides this relation of one being the knowledge of the other, a relation which we fix and retain for use, when once it is itself made objective to subsequent perception, by calling the subjective member of it, or knowledge, *objective thought,* and the objective member of it, or existence, *object thought of.* These latter terms are names of the obverse aspects, when these are themselves considered as being together the object of a subsequent perception. Both are objective; but the one, *objective thought,* is knowledge *qua* existent; the other, *object thought of,* is existence *qua* known to exist.

Here, then, we make our first halting place, mark off our first division, in methodical and philosophical thought,—at this distinction between the two ever inseparable but ever distinguishable companions, the subjective and objective aspects. Farther than this, as a first step, nothing warrants us in going. In fact, even in order to see whether the two aspects, which form an inseparable pair, stand in any further or still more intimate relation to each other, whether they are in any sense identical, or coalescent, or condition and conditionate, we must first have seen that they are distinguishable, though inseparable, and there for a moment pause. And this justifies us in establishing the *distinction of aspects* as the first great rubric, category, or division, of method; for it is evident, that everything without exception, from the universe to an atom, from the vaguest and largest thought, taken as an existent, to the smallest and minutest sensation, falls under this rubric, since it stands in this relation, and must so stand, or it would not for us exist at all, nor could we surmise it even in a dream.

B

Analysis of Elements.

Our first step in analysis having resulted in giving us the two aspects, both of them objective to reflection, what we have next to do is to apply again the same guiding principle of method to this result, and analyse it by putting to it the same question *What*. The two aspects are now our object-matter, instead of the world of empirical absolutes, the world of common sense and positive science, with which we began. We have still indeed, in one sense, the same world, the same facts, before us, but they are distributed and arranged differently. The limit-question about Being has thrown them into the crucible, and the answer to it has reproduced them in a new shape. The content of experience or of consciousness, which before appeared as the ordinary empirical world, now appears as a series or a system of objective thoughts, over against and representing, either item for item, or general outline for items unknown in detail, a series or a system of objects thought of; the former system containing what we know or imagine of the latter. For ultimately and in last resort, the meaning of which restriction will be seen more clearly as we proceed, we know nothing of the nature or whatness of objects thought of, save through objective thought, always of course taking *thought* as including perception and feeling, which are constituents of it. Just as Being generally is the object of reflective perception, and the two aspects perceived by that reflection are the whatness of Being, so, at this second stage of the analysis, the objects thought of are existents whose whatness is given in their obverse or subjective aspect, the objective thoughts corresponding to them.

Clearly, then, our immediate business is with the series or system of objective thoughts, as objects of reflection, and our business with it is to ask *what it is*, both in general and in detail, both in totals and in parts of totals; to ask what we immediately know it as being, or in other words, to analyse it for its whatness. And it is obvious, in the first place, that as a whole this inseparable aspect of Being, objective thought, cannot be characterised by anything not included in itself; cannot, therefore, be classified under any larger category, any more than (as remarked above) Being itself can. Its analysis, therefore, must consist in the observation, comparison, and classification, of differences and similarities within itself, of one part or feature of it with others, or of the various relations between them, the whole object-matter being taken to consist of *thoughts,* or states of consciousness in the widest sense of the term, but in no wis transcending consciousness or thought, which, as we have already seen, is a phrase aiming to express a contradiction as if it were non-contradictory. Accordingly I characterise this rubric, or division, of our enquiry as *analysis of elements,* meaning thereby the constituents or components, either of the content of objective thought in general, or of any objective thought taken singly, or again of any group of objective thoughts, whether more or less complex.

It is here that the proper work-a-day business of philosophy begins. It is under this rubric, that by far the larger as well as the more important part of it work is done. The former rubric contains work which clears the ground, secures the field, ascertains the scope, for the work to be done under this. What sort of Universe the world we live in makes part of, is a question which, in all its details, depends ultimately, for any solution we can obtain, upon the results of the analysis of objective thought under this rubric. It is this analysis that establishes the *premisses* for all conclusions in that matter. It is by this, that the very meaning of the terms, *universe, world,* and *life,* have to be ascertained. The question is, what do we immediately know of the objects provisionally designated, in common sense and in science, by these and other names of similar character. It is this that gives substance to the title *metaphysical* applied to philosophy, I mean the circumstance of its being the analysis of objective thought, which contains all we know of objects thought of, whether these are provisionally designated material or spiritual objects.

It would be entirely out of place to attempt to indicate here how, in my opinion, it is best to set to work in instituting this analysis, and still more to mention any, even the most general, results which I may suppose to have been obtained by its means. But I would desire, if possible, to make present to your minds the immense extent and richness of the field for that analysis, by recalling in general terms the provinces which it covers, and the contents of which it redistributes from its own point of view; that is to say, by taking them in their character of objective thoughts, or, as we may figuratively describe it, regarding them as composing one side of the same shield which has its other side turned towards common sense and positive science. I would remind you then, that *all* the phenomena belonging to *all* the departments of knowledge, however demarcated, belong equally and alike, in virtue of their subjective character, to this department of philosophy; that is to say, those belonging 1st to Logic, Ethic, Æsthetic, Mathematic, Theology; 2nd to Dynamics, Physics, Chemistry, Biology, Psychology; 3rd to the immense group of sciences of concrete human action, Sociology, Politic, Jurisprudence, Political Economy, Language, and many others; and lastly to the still more minute and complex subdivisions formed out of these or out of their interlacing ramifications, which it would be hopeless for me to enumerate.

I make no attempt at logical accuracy of classification. What I wish to bring home to you is, that nothing is excluded from the single all-embracing field of subjective analysis, but that this field singly covers, and is co-extensive with, the fields of all other departments of knowledge taken together, so far as those departments treat their several fields objectively, as objects thought of, and not as objective thoughts. A department which treats, or so far as it treats, its field of phenomena subjectively. Ethic, for instance, or Logic, is *eo ipso* a branch of philosophy, and has its roots in this department of it. The whole of experience, then, in its character of objective thought, falls under this subjective analysis; and, as the object-matter of that analysis, may be compared to a moving or changing panorama; an image which indeed is itself nothing but *pars pro toto;* visual objects, which are but a single class, being made to stand for all classes, or the whole content of consciousness. Moreover it must be remembered, not only that the field of philosophy embraces the whole of experience, but that in analysing it, or any part of it, we bring it again before us in the same manner in which it was experienced originally; that is to say, we are again looking at it through and in reflective perception; we repeat the act which is constitutive of experience, and is the constant feature in it, and which therefore, supposing it contributes anything to its objects, contributes equally and alike to all of them.

We have then a vast field, and an immense task, of analysis before us under this rubric, a task, however, upon which we are not now to enter. But the question must be asked,—supposing this task entered on, and accomplished by each of us in his own way, and so far as he may be able to accomplish it, how far is the analysis capable of being pushed, and what is the purpose, what the ultimate proposed limits, of the enquiry? The answer can only be, that the analysis must be pushed until we see two things, 1st the *de facto* order, both of co-existence and sequence, in which the objective thoughts have actually occurred and been brought together so as to compose our panorama in its largest extent, and 2nd the logical arrangement, co-ordination, and subordination, of those same objective thoughts into an organic whole, so that the relations between them may be expressed as general facts or laws, under which the particular objective thoughts are brought as cases or instances. The analysis of the panorama and all its parts will not be complete, until both these insights have been obtained. But how immeasurably remote that attainment is, hardly needs pointing out. If we had a perfect memory of the history of our thought from the first dawn of consciousness, we should have attained the first; if we had, besides this, perfect powers of discrimination and comparison, we should have attained the second; and this I say merely to show the extreme magnitude and complexity of the task.

For as it is, we are left to infer almost the whole of the first, by attending to those additions to the panorama, which have occurred since the time when we began to analyse it philosophically. And a knowledge of the first, at least to a very considerable extent, is an indispensable pre-requisite to the attainment of the second. No mere analysis of the panorama itself, or of its parts, as we have them before us at any single given time of philosophising, will give us a knowledge of the historical order in which the panorama itself, or any of its more complex parts, has been put together, by synthesis or amalgamation of part with part, in our consciousness, during the time of its development. And yet the history of the panorama in our consciousness is part and parcel of the panorama itself, in the large sense in which we have been understanding the term hitherto. We find the panorama, at any given time, not only as a given panorama, but as one which is then and there being added to, receiving new accretions, or as a process of increasing knowledge which is actually going on, making its own history. It is a moving or changing panorama; and its growth, or the genesis of its parts, is an essential feature in it.

The question of *genesis*, not indeed of the panorama as a whole, but of its parts, their *de facto* historical connection with each other, is thus raised. Here is the logical origin of that question; I mean the *locus* of the conception of *genesis* in the whole panorama of objective thought, which as a whole is our *analysandum*. The *de facto* connection of parts in historical order, which is part of the process or growth of the panorama, is as essential a constituent of the *analysandum*, as either the logical and generalised connection of parts, in any portion of the panorama which may have come into view in consequence of that process, or the specific content and quality of any part or group of parts which it embraces.

Moreover it will be noticed, that *genesis* of parts, the enquiry into which thus distinctly arises out of our analysis of the panorama of objective thought, is one member of the guiding distinction of our method,—the distinction between nature and genesis, conditions of essence and conditions of existence. The question is indeed put originally, and at present, only about objective thoughts, —how these severally arise and come into the panorama, —but the whole question of the nature of genesis everywhere is thereby opened. We began by adopting, as our principle of method, a distinction drawn between nature and genesis, as things the difference of which was provisionally known. But now we see, that genesis itself, as known to us in the panorama, is a fact which is subordinate to the fact of nature, or has itself a nature into which we are forced to enquire.

We find from analysing the panorama of objective thoughts, that there is a *de facto* order of co-existence and sequence in them, which is capable of being reduced, partially or wholly, to uniformity and regularity, and subsumed under general facts, or laws, of co-existence and sequence. The term *genesis* is a general name for it. But general names are never explanations of the facts which they cover. The explanation lies, if anywhere, in the facts as analysed, and not in the names which sum up the results of analysis. The question, *What makes* a given objective thought appear in the panorama at any particular juncture, or a given place in the panorama be occupied by an individual thought of specific and individualised quality, still remains. The name, whatever it be, which we give to the fact which we suppose will answer this question, is always a general name, and a general name only. Call it *energy,* or *agency,* or *will,* or *thought,* or *consciousness,* or *spirit,* or *Subject,* or *Object,* or the *Absolute,*—call it what you like,—still these names have no specific, individual, content; they are general names meaning *that which* makes, does, acts, produces, causes, generates, and so on,—*assuming* that there is *an agent* at work there, but a hidden agent. This hidden agent and agency, which appear to be at work in the panorama of consciousness, are what we want, if possible, to arrive at and ascertain. At any rate we want to ascertain whether they are ascertainable, and if not, why not; or, if they are an illusion, why they are illusory, and how the illusion arises. These are questions which we must be careful not to prejudge, or answer by assumptions, one way or the other. At this point, therefore, of philosophical enquiry, we close the department headed *analysis of elements,* and open our enquiry into the agency at work, by placing that enquiry under an entirely new rubric or title.

C

The Order of Real Conditioning.

Again we have a fresh start to make, again we have to review the present position of our philosophical enquiry as a whole, and again we have to apply our guiding principle of method. We closed the rubric of analysis of elements, because we found it unable to reveal the *de facto* order in which the history of its own object-matter had taken place in the past, and in which it is still taking place as we examine it. It does not follow that, supposing we obtain light on these points from elsewhere, the knowledge so obtained will not take its place and be incorporated into the total panorama of objective thought. Indeed this is the very result which we aim at. To obtain knowledge of anything is *eo ipso* to incorporate it into the panorama of objective thought. It was with this very purpose in view, that we dwelt upon the characteristics of objective thought itself, and particularly upon its demarcation from its own obverse aspect, object thought of, which was forced upon us by the very nature of the act of experiencing. We have now had some specific evidence for what was stated perhaps somewhat dogmatically at the outset, namely, that our whole knowledge of objects thought of comes in the form of objective thoughts, or that we know nothing of objects thought of *per se*, apart from our thoughts of them. *They, per se*, can afford us no explanation of objective thoughts, because except by objective thoughts they are totally unknown. And yet where else is it possible to look, for an enlargement of our knowledge of objective thoughts? This is our first question.

Now if we consider our present position in connection with the purpose of philosophy as a whole, we shall, I think, see at a glance the quarter to which we must turn. The purpose aimed at by philosophy, namely, a Rationale of the universe so far as attainable by man, includes a harmonising of the ordinary world of objects, as seen by common sense and positive science, with the world as seen by philosophy; which means, in other words, incorporating the results of common sense and positive science with the specifically philosophical results of subjective analysis of objective thoughts, which is a specifically philosophical rubric. Philosophy, as we saw, comes into being as the last in a series of three lines of thought, and starts from the basis afforded by the two earlier ones, the facts of experience as they are presented by common sense and positive science. The term has therefore both a narrower and a broader signification, according as it is considered either as contradistinguished by its method from common sense and positive science, or else as aiming at a harmony, to be established by itself, between itself and them; a harmony to be attained, not by using the results of science, as they stand at any given epoch, as unalterable criteria or tests of philosophical truth, as if both stood on the same footing, or were reached by the same method, but by so combining the results obtained from time to time by both, as mutually to illustrate and supplement each other.

It is therefore greatly to be wished, that philosophers should acquaint themselves, so far as practicable, with the methods and results of positive science, and men of science also, so far as practicable, with the method and results of philosophy. This is a view the very opposite of that which is unhappily but too prevalent at present on both sides, and more particularly opposed to that view of philosophy which conceives it, not only as totally and in its whole course independent of science, but even as called upon to prescribe *a priori* laws, and establish *a priori* delimitations, for science, within its own scientific domain.

Approaching, then, the question of real conditioning with such views as I have described, philosophy is met by the fact, which it learns from common sense and positive science, that real objects are always regarded by them as objects thought of, and not as combinations of objective thoughts. They do not put the question, *what the objects are known as;*—do not put it at all;—but, assuming that certain objects exist as realities, proceed at once to ask how they are produced, and how they behave. That is to say, taking certain combinations of objective thoughts as identical with objects thought of, they enter at once upon the order of real conditioning, to which, as objects thought of, they belong.

The next significant fact which philosophy learns from its new instructors is this,—and here we shall begin, if I mistake not, to see light,—that these real and concrete objects thought of have, as such, and in that character, another analysis, besides the subjective one into aggregates or combinations of objective thoughts, namely, an analysis into *other* objects thought of. This analysis is given by positive science in different branches, belonging to one or more of the general heads of Dynamics, Physics, Chemistry, Biology, and Psychology. Atoms, molecules, masses, ethers, gases, chemical compounds, living tissues, cells, minds, souls, or whatever may be the agents in conscious beings, and specific powers of mind or soul, *e.g.*, the will, and the reason, or other specific functions of organs in conscious beings; and also the modes in which all these are severally and respectively combined, and the modes of action proper to each severally, and in their respective combinations;—are all so many objects thought of,—which have indeed again an analysis into objective thoughts (or we could not lay hold of them, so to speak, in thought at all),—but which exist and operate, as there is abundant evidence taken from objective thought to show, quite independently of their subjective analysis into objective thoughts, and quite irrespective of our making or not-making that analysis.

We see, then, that there are some groups of objecti· thoughts which have a double analysis, one as objecti· thoughts into other objective thoughts, and one as objec thought of into other objects thought of. And not or so, but they behave quite differently in the two characte That is to say, the groups of objects thought of, given the one analysis, behave quite differently from the grou of objective thoughts given by the other. *Things,* in common language, behave quite differently from the *thoughts* about them. The two are torn asunder from each other, and localised differently; they are duplicated in point of space. Thoughts are localised in living bodies, that is, have a constant environment of a particular set of thoughts, called (as object thought of) a body. But the things thought of by those thoughts, other than the body and its parts, which is their constant environment, are localised in space outside the body, and form a total which is called the material world. And not only so, but it is found also, that the occurrences of thoughts depend, in many instances, upon the existence of things which are not the objects thought of by them, but follow laws and sets of laws of their own, as things and not as thoughts.

For instance, the occurrence, say, of a thunderstorm last night, which is analysable into a group of objective thoughts, is not traceable to any other objective thoughts which have either previously or simultaneously occurred as parts of my system of experience, but to the occurrence of certain objects of thought, whether thought of or not at or before the occurrence of the thunderstorm, but which, like the thunderstorm, can be analysed into groups of objective thoughts. Nothing ultimately and in the last resort (as was said above) escapes analysis into objective thoughts; but not only does this fact fail to explain the occurrence of objective thoughts, in that order of coexistence and sequence in which they occur actually, but on the contrary the occurrence of objective thoughts depends, at least in instances like the foregoing, both upon the existence of objects thought of, and upon their occurrence, not only to conscious beings, but also *inter se,* or to each other, independently of their occurrence to conscious beings.

Now it is undeniable that, in bringing together these two worlds, of things and of thoughts about things, philosophy is only bringing together things which belong to its own first and second rubrics, objective thoughts and objects thought of, inasmuch as all objects thought of have an analysis into objective thoughts, and are unknowable otherwise. Separated as these now are into two different worlds, each following its own laws, philosophy still brings them together under its first and second rubrics, and indeed, in the second rubric, as knowable things, under the single category of objective thoughts. Yet it has not thereby, as at first sight it might seem to do, contradicted its own assertion, that objects thought of are knowable only in the form of objective thoughts, and by so doing transcended the world of phenomena, and laid claim to a knowledge of the unknowable, or of things-in-themselves, which are nothing but the objectivity of objects thought of taken alone, or the bare thought of existence hypostasised as an object. For the objects now thought of are not so many cases of the mere obverse aspect of objective thoughts taken alone, but are objects of common sense and positive science, that is, are objects which are already, as such, in the form of objective thoughts, though they are also treated by common sense and by positive science (*but not by philosophy*) as if they were *only* objects thought of, and not also objective thoughts. It is common-sense and scientific thought which omits to notice, that the double aspect is essential to all phenomena, and which consequently treats its objects as if they belonged to the objective aspect alone,—an aspect which philosophy shows to involve a contradiction, when isolated in that fashion.

Philosophy, therefore, makes a great change in the objects of common sense and positive science, when it *takes* them up into its own system; and the change consists in stripping them of their *absolute* character, while retaining their concrete and empirical character; that is, it continues to treat them as concrete and empirical, but ceases to regard them as absolute existents. Stated briefly the case is this,—what philosophy seeks in the objects, which common sense and positive science treat as and call objects thought of, is the filling up, the detail, the individualised content, not of its own category of object thought of,—which would be contradictory,—but of some general term, or terms, included in its own objective thought, namely, those of genesis, cause, real conditioning, energy, and the like.

The term *object thought of* has, therefore. a different meaning, in this third rubric of philosophy, both from its meaning in common sense and positive science, out of which it drops the absolutism, and from its meaning in the second rubric of philosophy, out of which it drops the character of being a purely logical abstraction, namely, bare abstract existence. Similarly, and simultaneously, the corresponding term *objective thought* assumes a changed meaning, by dropping out of its former meaning the real conditioning or real genesis of the content, which was before included in it, but only as covered and expressed by general terms. This part of its former meaning has now passed over to the term which is its opposite, but which no longer expresses its *obverse* aspect,—namely, *object thought of*. A Chimæra, for instance, is a group of objective thoughts. Its obverse aspect, or object thought of, in the sense of the second rubric, is the Chimæra as existent. But its object thought of, in the sense of the present third rubric, is that set of real conditions, be they what they may, which produce the objective thought *Chimæra* in consciousness.

Philosophy, therefore, in bringing these two things together in their changed meanings, has also brought them together in a changed relation, that of real condition and conditionate. We see moreover that, while all real conditions are both objective thoughts and objects thought of, in the old meaning of these terms, it does not follow, that all objective thoughts with their objects thought of, in the old meaning, are real conditions, or objects thought of in the new meaning, the Chimæra for instance. Objective thoughts are now conditionates of objects thought of; and objects thought of are now real conditions, both of each other and of objective thoughts. The question, then, which we now have to consider is, what or rather which kinds of objective thoughts with their objects thought of,—that is, objective thoughts taken as existents,—in the old sense of the terms, are capable of being, or actually are, real conditions of others; that is, are objects thought of, in the new sense of the present rubric; and which kinds, on the other hand, are objective thoughts only, or are what common sense and positive science call mere creatures of the mind.

The difference between the strictly philosophical and the strictly scientific meaning of the terms *objective thought* and *object thought of* arises solely from a difference of starting point and method. Science begins by assuming the existence of real objects, and then immediately puts the question of their genesis and behaviour, while philosophy asks what is meant by their existence. In the case of external objects actually perceived, the object thought of, which science contemplates, is thus not only a real condition of itself as at that time known, that is, of the objective thought which is its obverse aspect, but it is much more besides,—a perfect mine of surprises for the investigator. All these are covered by the assumption of its existence as a real condition, inasmuch as they are included in its reality as an existent, with properties as yet unknown. Science leaves this assumption unexamined, in putting the question of genesis before the question, what its objects are for consciousness. To put that question first, is to assume the real existence of a whole army of properties, which may or may not come into knowledge afterwards; and this assumption of real but unknown existents, which are also real conditions, is therefore involved in the first principle of scientific method. Philosophy on the other hand, in asking simply what existence means, discovers the fact in consciousness, that every existent, or property of an existent, whether positively known or only assumed, has its objective thought, by which knowledge, as it were, lays hold of it, an objective thought which is not the conditionate, but the obverse aspect, of the existent known or assumed to exist. The logical transition from the one point of view to the other, and consequent proof of the compatibility of their results, are what has to be effected in detail by philosophy, under this its third rubric.

Here accordingly we apply again our guiding distinction of philosophical method, by putting the question *what* to real conditions. What is *meant by* a real condition, what is the *nature* of it? And we intend, of course, by this question, what is that, in any object thought of, which gives it, or in which consists, what we call generally conditioning power? What *specifically* is *that which* makes, causes, does, produces, or determines anything? What *specifically* are agency, energy, power, force, and so on? We have taken positive science into council on this question, because positive science has made the study of real conditions specifically taken its peculiar province. Disregarding generalities, it fixes its attention upon the analysis of individual concrete things into their actual individual components, upon things as perceived, instead of things as conceptually generalised. Here then, if anywhere, we may expect aid towards finally answering our great question, What is Being, and making a step onwards towards a Rationale of the sum of things.

The clue followed must of course be the distinction between objects thought of and objective thought, in the sense of this third rubric, which in other words is the distinction between real conditions, as empirical objects with a partially known content, and objective thoughts taken simply as existing in consciousness alone, and not as the obverse aspect of the real conditions which may be in question. We thus follow the line of thought followed by positive science. But there is one among the positive sciences, which stands in a peculiarly close connection with philosophy, inasmuch as it has objective thought as part of its special object-matter. I mean of course psychology, which treats of the genesis of consciousness, or of consciousness in connection with its real conditions; that is, in connection, not with objects thought of in their whole range, but with those which are the real conditions of objective thoughts.

Following, then, the line of scientific thought, in which real conditions are taken in fusion with, and undistinguished from, the objective thoughts which are their obverse aspect, and at the same time separated in thought from the objective thoughts which they condition, the first distinction, which we observe between them, is into those conditions of consciousness which are internal, and those which are external, to the body of the conscious Subject; *the body*, as already noted, being the name for that set of objective thoughts, treated as an object thought of, which is the constant environment of consciousness, the object constantly present to it, at the centre of its field of vision, whatever other objects are present or absent. Those real conditions of consciousness which are internal to the body are called provisionally its proximate conditions, those which are external its remote conditions. I say provisionally, to mark that I am here speaking only of the first step from common sense to science; for we find, that science afterwards restricts the proximate conditions within the narrower bounds of the nerve and brain system. In this way it is, that psychology, as a positive science, approaches the question of the genesis of consciousness, and this approach to it is in perfect harmony with the general system of philosophy.

And here it must be noticed, that the question of genesis is thus proposed in its greatest extent and comprehensiveness. It was raised originally, in the second rubric, as a question within the limits of consciousness, a question concerning the genesis of parts within the panorama of objective thought, that is, of some parts out of others, and not concerning the genesis of the whole panorama. But now it is seen, that the question concerns the whole, just as much as it concerns the parts; for it appears, from considerations belonging to common sense and positive science, that a concrete conscious being is, everywhere and always, one at least of the indispensable real conditions of changes in the panorama of consciousness; and, since all consciousness, consciousness itself, includes, requires, or partly consists of change, it necessarily follows, that a concrete conscious being is also an indispensable real condition of consciousness altogether.

But though the question of genesis concerns the whole as much as it concerns the parts, it does not concern it in the same way. The moment it is put concerning the genesis of the panorama of objective thoughts as a single whole, it is put concerning its real existence; but its real existence has hitherto been pre-supposed, including that of its parts, as the *object perceived* under the first rubric; and this real existence is expressed, under the second rubric, as the object, or objects, thought of; which objects are known in no other way save in the form of objective thoughts. Consequently, there is either no answer possible to the question concerning the genesis of the panorama as a single whole, since its object thought of *is* its real existence, and cannot at the same time be the real condition or cause of its existence, that is, of itself; or else the concrete conscious being, or beings, which we have now seen to be among the indispensable real conditions of the panorama as a whole, are conditions of it in a different way, or different respect, from that in which some parts within it have been hitherto taken as conditions of others. Concrete conscious beings are themselves concrete existents forming part of the whole panorama. And therefore the whole panorama seems to depend, for its genesis or existence as a reality, upon concrete existents which have no other real existence than as parts of the panorama dependent upon other parts of it.

We are thus led by our method itself, and the system which is its development, to bring up for solution those very questions which were expressly noticed above, in speaking of a certain ambiguity which I described as lying across the very threshold of philosophy, and which were then expressly reserved for future investigation;— I mean the questions concerning the nature of the Subject of consciousness or thought, and the nature of its Object; that is, the nature of the Subject taken as an object among objects, but contradistinguished from the rest of them. It is from common sense and positive science that these notions are originally derived, and therefore it is inevitable that they should come forward for investigation, when the general view taken by common sense and positive science comes forward for incorporation into the philosophical system. And the solution will be found, if anywhere, in that transformation in the meaning of the terms *objective thought* and *object thought of,* which has just above been described.

From this it will appear that, as all objects thought of are now identified with concrete real conditions, so all objective thoughts must also be identified with the panorama of objective thought *minus* its real conditions; and therefore that Subjects and Objects, as real conditions of each other and of consciousness, must be conceived as the real conditions, not of the whole world of consciousness or thought including the real existence of its objects, but of the whole world of consciousness or thought as contradistinguished from the reality of its objects. In other words, the genesis of consciousness as a whole is a scientific and psychological question, as distinguished from a metaphysical one; and its solution depends upon our acquiring a scientific knowledge of the nature of the Subject, as a real existent and real condition, and also of the laws of its interaction with other objects which are real in the same sense of the term. The alternative conception is one which is alike absurd in common sense and self-contradictory in logic, namely, that the individual Subject, or every individual Subject, if more than one, is at once unknowable and the author of the whole of Nature.

Our third philosophical rubric may now, I think, be regarded as fairly established, and its logical position sufficiently justified. It will not be expected of me in this case, any more than under the second rubric, to enter upon any substantive treatment of its problems, or to indicate what I may conceive as results obtained, or likely to be obtained hereafter, by pursuing them. My present business is solely to exhibit the articulation of the system of philosophy, so far as it depends on the principle of method which it adopts. But another question, similar to one asked in the previous case, must also be asked in this, namely, what are the ultimate scope and limits of the enquiry, and how far is the analysis of real conditions to be pushed? The answer here is very simple. It is to be pushed as far as the positive sciences, one and all, can push it. It has no other scope and limits but theirs. Their results are what it is desired to incorporate into a philosophical system. It is the interest of philosophy to take up these results simply as science gives them, unaltered by any bias, or by assumptions derived from a philosophical source. One change, and one only, philosophy makes, which is indeed the necessary condition of incorporating them,—the abandonment of the absolute character attached by imagination to the objects thought of, an abandonment which, I think, no man of science will hesitate to make, the moment his attention is fairly drawn to its meaning and purport.

[Let* us see what it means in the case of the physical sciences. Its meaning is, that we cannot know of Matter, that is, of any material object, process, or mode of action, without having it in some way present to thought or imagination, whether by means of symbols or otherwise. In other words, everything is relative to knowledge, or has a subjective aspect. And the value of this for philosophy, as a means of incorporating the results of science into a philosophical system, consists in the fact, that our conceptions of the ultimate elements, or ultimate laws, of the material world, which have this subjective aspect, are always liable to the question *what we mean* by them, what the elements or laws are definitely known or imagined as being; whereby it is seen, whether they are capable of a further analysis in thought or not. It thus secures us against too readily acquiescing in any view of matter and material processes as ultimate, when it is not really

* The part within brackets, down to the words—*now been combating, was omi*tted for brevity's sake in delivery.

pushed to the furthest degree of minuteness attainable, though it may be practically sufficient for immediate scientific needs, on the plea that the real nature of everything is transcendent, or that *Things-in-themselves*, though existent, are unknowable.

Turning to psychological science, the meaning, and therefore also the practicability, of the abandonment is less plain. Psychology is the science which has one half of its object-matter, I mean consciousness, in common with philosophy; the difference consisting in the way in which this object-matter is treated by each respectively. Psychology treats it in respect of its genesis, philosophy in respect of its analysis. Yet psychology also analyses it, though only in relation to its real conditions, while philosophy analyses its content generally, without this restriction. This gives rise to complications, which make it less easy for psychologists frankly to abandon the absolute character of the real condition of consciousness, taken as a whole. I mean, of course, by the real condition of consciousness as a whole, our old friend the Subject. The difficulty is this:—if consciousness as a whole, including every part or every thought which it contains, depends upon the Subject, how can the Subject be liable to the question, *what we mean* by it, since its meaning must consist in a thought, or thoughts, in consciousness, which in *all* its thoughts depends upon the Subject? It seems, then, that the Subject at least, whatever may be the case with objects, is necessarily transcendent, that is, prior to and independent of consciousness altogether, including even its most general thought, the relation of objectivity and subjectivity; or in other words, that it exists in itself, out of and beyond all relations of thought, as the condition generating thought itself, and therefore the prior condition of any relation of thought existing at all. If, then, the Subject is the real condition of consciousness, and is itself unknowable, as having no possible meaning in terms of consciousness, it follows that we are precluded from any real knowledge of how consciousness is conditioned, and psychology becomes a science without an object, its object-matter being shared between an *a priori* philosophy of the Absolute, on one side, and a mere registration of unreal phenomena, on the other.

Psychologists are therefore in this dilemma, either to abandon this reasoning which robs their science of its knowable object-matter, or to admit that the Subject is an empirical and concrete object among objects, the laws of whose action are open to scientific investigation. If what has been said above, under the present rubric, holds good, their judgment cannot long remain in suspense. For we have now the means of detecting the fallacy of one of the alternatives. The premiss of the reasoning, which makes the Subject an unknowable absolute, is ambiguous. The premiss is, that consciousness in all its parts, or thoughts, depends upon the Subject. But this, which is true, when consciousness, of which it is said, is taken as a term of already ascertained meaning, is tacitly understood to imply what is false, namely, that consciousness, the meaning of which has been left unascertained, depends upon the Subject for its nature, and for the nature of its thoughts, as well as for their genesis. This tacit assumption empties consciousness of its content in every respect, and leaves it a non-entity. Whereas we have seen, that the question of genesis cannot and does not arise concerning a non-entity, and consequently that consciousness, when the question of genesis is asked concerning it, cannot mean less than the series or panorama of objective thoughts, taken simply as a series of occurrences, having indeed a nature of their own, but abstracting from their relation to the objects thought of, which are their obverse aspect.

Similarly we saw, that those things only which are already known as real existents, and have already a meaning in consciousness, can be held to be real conditions of anything else. The Subject, therefore, is a particular object thought of; and to transfer to it *in potentia* the whole content of consciousness indiscriminately is to rob it of its own particular content, contrary to the conditions of the problem. In truth, the fact that what we know as consciousness, which in its lowest form is simply feeling, sentience, or awareness, and has no other definition but a name, arises in the Subject,— this fact is due proximately to the existence and operation of the Subject itself; the Subject being at the same time taken as a real existent, with a nature already partly known to us who reason about it, though not necessarily to itself while giving rise to consciousness. And the question which we have, if possible, to answer in psychology is, what specifically is that feature or characteristic in the Subject, upon the existence of which, in any of its forms, consciousness in any of its forms comes into existence. The root of the fallacy in the reasoning, which makes the Subject an unknowable absolute, lies in forgetting to ask *what is meant* by consciousness, before proceeding to put the question of its genesis. In every case of genesis, both the conditionate and its condition must have some ascertained content or meaning, if the genesis of the conditionate is to be discovered. Its nature cannot be surrendered, or transferred to its condition in the character of a cause, without reducing the question of its genesis to an absurdity.

Accordingly, the true relation between consciousness and the Subject is, that the Subject depends upon consciousness, not for its genesis, but for its knowledge of its own nature, while consciousness depends upon the Subject for its genesis, but not for its nature, which, as we saw under the first rubric, is something *per se notum*, the ultimate or most original thing in knowledge. Moreover the distinction which lies at the basis of all further discrimination of their respective functions, and thereby enables us to demarcate with accuracy the provinces of philosophy and psychology, is one which was also brought out in our first rubric, as common and essential to all distinct consciousness, I mean the distinction between *whatness* and *thatness*, a distinction which runs down, so to speak, right through the middle both of consciousness itself, and of all objects of consciousness, of whatever kind. On this distinction the whole question of genesis depends, inasmuch as it belongs and relates only to the objective aspect of experience; because we must first know or assume *that* a thing *exists*, before we can put the question, *how it comes*, or *how it behaves*. But this does not prevent our asking, on what consciousness itself depends, because we logically can, and actually do, take consciousness as an existent, in asking the question. Our great distinction of method, between nature and genesis, is therefore applicable even to consciousness, but only in virtue of *whatness* and *thatness* being a distinction which is universally found in consciousness itself.

Now we have already placed, as it were, consciousness as conditionate, and the Subject as its real condition, over against each other. On the one hand we have states and changes of states of consciousness in all their manifold variety, on the other we have states and changes of states of the Subject, in a variety corresponding point for point with the former. But the states and changes of either series have both a whatness and a thatness, and it is with their thatness alone that real conditioning has immediately to do. The thatness of those in consciousness depends on the thatness of those in the Subject; and in this *de facto* dependence the real conditioning of consciousness by the Subject consists. The whatness of the states and changes in the two series is only a means of knowing the fact of their correspondence with each other, since they correspond in point of whatness, as well as in point of sequence or simultaneity of occurrence. But the correspondence, in point of whatness, of the states and changes of states belonging to the two series, is not identity. If they were identical in the point of whatness, as well as concomitant in occurrence, they would be related as obverse aspects to each other, and not as condition and conditionate. But as it is, the whatness of a state or change of state in consciousness is not the whatness of the corresponding state or change in the Subject. The two series are thus essentially heterogeneous. It is necessary to dwell somewhat longer on this point.

The essential feature which runs throughout consciousness, and serves to differentiate it from its real condition, is what has been already mentioned as feeling, sentience, or awareness. No object thought of possesses this characteristic, as an object simply. Subjects possess it, not in their character of objects thought of, that is, as a part of their own content as objects, but as the *bearers* of it, that is, as being the real conditions in which, and in dependence upon whose action, it arises and is maintained. There is therefore a fundamental heterogeneity between Subjects and their consciousness. But it is a heterogeneity which is discovered only when we begin to compare the two aspects of concrete existents, or of the panorama of consciousness, in respect of their share in the order of real conditioning, and put the question of genesis to the series of objective thoughts separated in thought from objects thought of, which, as we have seen, is work belonging to our present third rubric. The difference between objects which are possessed of sentience and those which are not is one familiar to common sense, and

E

fully recognised by science. But that this difference involves and pre-supposes a heterogeneity between the objects possessing and the sentience possessed, is a thought which arises only when we bring together into one view our analysis of objects, simply as known, and their relations to their conditions and conditionates. The first we see clearly, that the possession of sentience is a relation between things, each of which has a nature and analysis of its own, and definitely remove sentience from the analysis of the Subject *per se.* If the Subject is sentient, then it is not sentience. If on the other hand it is sentience, then it is not condition but conditionate. Life is a mode of motion in organisms, inherent in their substance, and therefore belongs solely to biology. But consciousness is not a mode of motion; it is changing sentience; dependent on life, but different from that on which it depends, and which in relation to it we call its Subject. And accordingly, consciousness does not belong solely to psychology, which treats of this relation, but is also the object-matter of another department of knowledge, which treats of it in its nature, namely, of philosophy.

Taking sentience, then, as the *differentia* of consciousness, as conditionate, from its real condition, we shall find that this differentia runs through the whole of it, and is the ground of its difference from the Subject in point of whatness. The simple qualities of feeling, as such, are something different in kind from the objects, or properties of objects, which give rise to them. Hardness to touch, for instance, is different as a feeling from hardness as a property of bodies. Resistance to pressure likewise. As properties of bodies, they are properties of things which are objects of thought and inference, as much as of sense. Nor does it in the least signify, whether *the objects,* to which these and similar properties, and the motions, tensions, and interactions depending on them, inherently belong, are objects external to the nerve organism, or are parts or properties internal to it; I mean supposing it to be the proximate real condition of consciousness. In every case, they are different in kind from the feelings, of which they are the immediate conditions.

The difference is still more obvious in the case of sensations of sight. The sensations of *red* and *blue*, for instance, have no resemblance to the vibrations or other motions in the organ of sight, on the occurrence of which they arise as sensations. I need not multiply instances. The same may be said of all feelings which have a distinguishable quality, including feelings of pleasure and pain, emotions, desires, and what are called feelings of action, to which belong sense of effort and volition. These are, if possible, still more unlike anything which we can imagine in the Subject as their immediate condition.

Again, even those properties of states and changes of states of consciousness which are quantitative, I mean degree of intensity, or strength, or vividness in feeling, relative duration, relative magnitude or volume, and relative place in mental imagery, are not the same as the corresponding properties in the states and changes of states which are their conditions. They only vary in correspondence with them.

Thus the two series are fundamentally heterogeneous throughout, but there is a close correspondence between their changes, both in point of actual concomitance, and in the quantitative properties, by the aid of which that actual concomitance is made known to us. We see, therefore, that it is not the whatness of the one series which depends either upon the whatness, or upon the thatness, of the other; but the *existence* of the one whatness upon the *existence* of the other. In putting the question of genesis, both the condition and the conditionate must be taken simply as existents, but without robbing them of their content; that is to say, the *de facto* existence of the concrete and empirical states and changes in the one is the condition of the *de facto* existence of the concrete and empirical states and changes in the other.

Strictly speaking, therefore, the states and changes of states in the Subject explain nothing in the corresponding states and changes in consciousness, but their coming into, continuing in, and vanishing from, the panorama of objective thought. And it is upon the occurrence of the former that the occurrence of the latter is conditioned. Moreover, since the Subject stands in close connection and interaction with external Nature, upon whose states and changes of states its own are conditioned, it is plain, that consciousness also is thereby brought into a mediate but assured dependence upon the external world.

And it should also be noted, that it signifies nothing to the foregoing argument, what hypothesis we make as to the nature of the Subject; that is, whether we take it to be the nerve organism, or some fine etherial matter in nerve or brain, or even to be an immaterial substance in unison with them, provided only it be a real existent, and not merely a logical abstraction made by imagination out of the abstract *Whatness* of consciousness, as *Things-in-themselves* are made out of its abstract *Thatness*. I would only observe that, if an immaterial substance is the hypothesis adopted, the heterogeneity between its states and changes and those of consciousness is rather increased than lessened, owing to the extreme difficulty, to say the least, of imagining in what its states and changes of states can consist. I place an immaterial substance, commonly known as a Soul or Mind, among possible hypo*theses*, not because I can myself throw it into an intelligible shape, but in order, by taking an extreme case, to include all hypotheses, concerning the nature of the Subject, which are really conceivable, and therefore within the limits of positive science. It is not against any positive mode of conceiving the Subject, however adventurous, that I have now been arguing, but against conceiving it as an absolute existent, a conception which would remove it from the range of science altogether, and make psychology a creature of *a priori* speculation.— On the whole, I think it may be held, in view of the foregoing considerations, that the real conditioning of the existence of consciousness, its states, and its changes, by or upon the existence of a corresponding series of states and changes in the Subject, as a real but not absolute existent, is the only true province of psychology.

This position I will endeavour to make clear by means of a simile, which however is not to be taken as more than an illustration of it. Suppose a candle brought at night into some vast hall, lighted, and then left to burn itself out. And let this represent the conscious life of a man from birth to death. The hall, with whatever it contains, is the world; the space outside is the rest of the universe; the candle is the Subject; the light of the candle is consciousness or knowledge; the objects seen in the sphere which it illumines are the contents of consciousness or the knowledge of objects; the darkness left unillumined is the unknown region beyond positive knowledge.

Now just as light reveals three things, itself, and objects, and darkness, so consciousness reveals itself, and the known, and the unknown; that is, it reveals the fact of the existence, and something of the nature, of all three. And just as the light of the candle depends for its existence upon the existence of the candle, so consciousness depends for its existence upon the existence of the Subject. And just as the revelation of the objects in the illumined sphere depends for its taking place upon the candle being lighted, and lasts until the candle is burnt out, so the taking place, or genesis, of our knowledge of objects depends upon the life, and lasts until the death, of the Subject. And as the light reveals the existence and something of the nature of the candle, so consciousness reveals the existence and something of the nature of the Subject. The candle is one of the objects revealed by its own light; the Subject is one of the objects revealed by its own consciousness. And the Subject's consciousness may well depend for its existence upon the existence of the Subject, just as the light of the candle depends for its existence on that of the candle.—Finally, as the existence and nature of the objects in the illumined sphere, and in the darkness beyond, are independent of the candle being lighted and illumining them, so the objects which are known by consciousness, both those within the range of positive knowledge, and those surmised beyond it, are or may be, in point of their existence, independent both of the Subject's life, and of the existence of the Subject's knowledge. They are at least conceived by the Subject as lasting much longer than his own life, and the existence of his own knowledge of them. A single moment of the existence of knowledge may have an indefinitely long duration as its object, just as a single moment of sight may cover immeasurable distances in space.

Psychology deals with the connection between the existence and nature of the Subject, on one side, and the existence and nature of his consciousness on the other; philosophy, as contradistinguished from psychology, with the connection between his consciousness and its objects. And the fact in philosophy, that the Subject's knowledge *of* himself forms part of his total knowledge of objects, no more clashes with the fact in psychology, that the existence of both parts of his knowledge depends on his own existence, than the fact, that the candle is one of the objects revealed by its own light, clashes with the fact, that the existence of the light, whatever it reveals, depends on the existence of the candle. Supposing the candle and its light were a conscious being and his consciousness, the candle would be conscious of its own existence solely by means of its own light; and yet its consciousness would depend entirely on its own prior existence as a candle. This latter point, in the case of the candle, we have means of knowing, as spectators *ab extra*, although to the candle itself it might be doubtful; just as we see, that the corresponding point in the real case of our own consciousness has been doubted, and still leads some psychologists to surmise a transcendent Subject to explain it.

I must warn you that I do not bring forward this illustration as an argument against that form of Idealism which is founded on this transcendental hypothesis, but only to show that we are not logically compelled to make or admit that hypothesis. I am not now engaged in proving against Idealists, that the reality of the world of objects other than the Subject, is a reality independent of the reality of the Subject, but only that the Subject's phenomenal reality is independent of a supposed transcendental reality in the Subject. The question now before us is not whether the Subject, taken either as transcendent or as phenomenal, creates its world of objects by perceiving them; but whether, supposing all other objects of thought to have a wholly knowable and relative reality, the Subject can logically think of its own reality as wholly knowable and relative also, or on the contrary is compelled to think of it as an absolute existence. In short, I am not now arguing the question of this form of Idealism; though I do not deny, that Idealism in both its forms, since the one leads necessarily to the other, is the natural consequence of taking the Subject as a non-phenomenal, or transcendent and absolute existent. I am standing at the point of view of psychology as a positive science, and wish from that point of view to make evident, that the conception of the Subject, or conscious being, as a real and operative, but not a transcendent or absolute, existent, in fact as the proximate real condition, without which his consciousness would not exist, is in perfect accordance with the fact, that his knowledge of himself is amenable to the criteria, because it shares the nature, of every other part of his knowledge.

In passing from the analysis of consciousness, under the second rubric, to its genesis under the third, we pass from the consideration of it in its generality, or as embracing all knowledge, to the consideration of it as a particular consciousness depending upon a particular Subject. But since *generality* and *particularity* are terms liable to great misunderstanding, a word or two is requisite to give precision to the foregoing statement.

Examining the nature of anything by simple analysis is a process which abstracts from the consideration of whether or not there are similar instances, which would give the same or similar results in analysis. Supposing a number of similar instances to exist, their analyses would be similar and the analysis made for one would apply, with certain differences, to the rest. The single analysis would have general applicability, in case the similar instances really existed; but the analysis alone says nothing of their real existence. Now it is such an analysis which we have supposed the Subject to make of his own consciousness, under our second rubric. We have supposed him to abstract from the fact, that he is a particular Subject of a particular consciousness, inasmuch as this is a piece of common-sense knowledge, and he begins to philosophise with the question, *What is Being*, simply. Since we start from a common-sense and not an *a priori* basis, there is nothing which can justify us in supposing, that the consciousness which we analyse, and in which the meaning of *Being* is the first question, is either other people's consciousness, or a world-consciousness. Nature has provided that, as a matter of fact, it is our own particular consciousness. But we abstract from our common-sense knowledge of this fact, in instituting a philosophical analysis of it.

The analysis, therefore, is one which would apply generally, but with certain differences, to the consciousness of similar Subjects, supposing them to exist. But of their real existence, or existence as real conditions, the analysis alone says nothing. The Subject knows them, as he knows himself, only in the form of objective thoughts in the content of his own consciousness; and he knows himself only as the real condition of his own consciousness, and not of theirs. If they are taken as real existents, they are and must be taken also as the real conditions each of his own consciousness. Although, therefore, the analysis of a single consciousness, which we have supposed to be made under our second rubric, has general applicability to other cases, yet it is not its generality in this sense from which we have passed, in passing from the second to the third rubric, because generality in this sense has not entered into the consideration of the second rubric at all. It is rather to than from generality, in this sense, that we have passed.

But there is another sense in which the term *generality* truly applies to the content analysed, in which its meaning is more liable to be confused with that of its opposite *particularity*, and the particular existence which falls under it. The content of consciousness has been spoken of above as a whole including all its parts, or all its thoughts. Now, although all its thoughts are also parts of it, yet a different relation to each other, and to the whole, is indicated by the name *thoughts*, namely, their common relation to consciousness in its whatness, as their *summum genus*. Thoughts are parts which have, or are considered as having, relations to other parts besides those which precede, accompany, or follow them, in actual historical order of suggestion; that is, other relations to the rest of consciousness than relations of position in order of time. They are therefore modifications, or differentiations, as well as simply parts, of consciousness. Consciousness is common to all, as well as divided into all. Its generality consists in the former relation, its particularity in the latter. It is from the generality to the particularity of consciousness, in this sense of the terms, that we have passed, in passing from the second to the third rubric. Everything that falls under *whatness* belongs to the first, everything that falls under *thatness* to the second. All existence, even the existence of consciousness, falls under the *thatness* of consciousness. And therefore, in taking the whole of consciousness as an existent, which we do in the third rubric, we take it both as a logical particular, as a particular instance of thatness, and also in its own particularity, or as consisting of parts, which in its case are thoughts occurring in succession, but not excluding the possibility of some occurring simultaneously with others in the succession.

It is only in this sense of consciousness, namely, as a particular existent, consisting of parts succeeding or accompanying one another in a time series, that consciousness can be a conditionate, or can be held to depend upon its Subject. Consciousness is then one particular existent, and the Subject is another, both being objects of consciousness in that larger sense of the term, in which it has a *nature,* which includes both a *whatness* and *thatness,* as set forth in our first rubric. This is the logical justification for what we have already found consonant with facts; namely, that on the one hand the Subject, as an object among objects, is the proximate real condition of the genesis of consciousness, as a single series of states and changes, and on the other, that groups of states and changes in consciousness constitute a knowledge of the Subject, but in no way generate or give rise to it. And therefore, unless we avowedly stand on a basis of *a priori* assumptions, it is sheer confusion of thought to hold, either that consciousness is the real condition of the Subject, on the plea that the Subject is known only in consciousness, or that the Subject, as the real condition of consciousness, must exist as an absolute, beyond consciousness altogether. For, as to the first point, the only priority which consciousness has over existence is merely a logical priority in knowledge; and as to the second, some positive knowledge of a thing, as an existent simply, is logically pre-supposed in knowledge of it as the real condition of any other thing.

If these points are granted, then it will follow, that the positive sciences, one and all, will form part of a great philosophical system, yet without losing an iota of their scientific independence and autonomy. It is no part of science, but only a bit of bad philosophy, which they are called on to abandon, in abandoning that form of absolutism which I have now been combating.]

Abandoning it they will enter the philosophical system on the footing, not of being prescribed to, but of prescribing. Philosophy, in my view, asks nothing better than to take up whatever results science may arrive at, and assigns to them, for that purpose, a special department or rubric in its own system.

But there is still a further question. Supposing that positive science abandons this form of absolutism, and that philosophy fairly accepts its guidance to the utmost attainable limits, can we say what and where those limits are; or more precisely, whether any final solution, which can be conceived as attainable by scientific methods, is of a nature to include within it all possible knowledge? Granting that there will always be a vast interval between the utmost knowledge, which we may hope to attain actually, and any such final solution, ideally comprehensive of all possible problems, as we have now in view; granting that there will always be a broad penumbra of the unexplored; still the question must be put, whether the ideally final solution, whatever its particular character may be, can embrace the Sum of Things, or whether we must conceive, that there are modes of existence beyond its range, which it does not embrace at all?

Now at first sight it seems, that some final solution, which shall ideally be all-embracing, must be conceivably attainable on these scientific lines, for the question of genesis has been put concerning the whole panorama of objective thought exhibited under our second rubric, and there shown to embrace the whole of its own obverse aspect, the whole object thought of; and then, under our present third rubric, the whole of this panorama has been redistributed into real conditions and conditionates, so that no corner of the whole is left, ideally, out of account or unexplained. Every part within the limits of the whole panorama has had the question of genesis, ideally speaking, asked and answered concerning it. And if we cannot put the question of genesis again concerning the nature of the panorama, that is to say, concerning the panorama and its objects thought of taken together, as a single whole, this circumstance, it may be said, only shows that a *scienti*fic analysis of the whole, when combined with a subjective or philosophical analysis of the whole, which is what we are now supposing to have been virtually accomplished, is the final solution, beyond which no solution can be expected only because, and for the very reason that, no question or problem can arise beyond it.

Certain current forms of such scientific solutions, it may also be said by those who take this view, may indeed have to be abandoned as inadequate. As for instance, the physicist's hypothesis of Matter and its physical forces or energies, or something analogous to it, as the primæval source and permanent substrate of all other forms of existence. Or again the psychologist's hypothesis of a single vast conscious being or Mind, producing and sustaining all things, and ordering them by some preconceived design, for purposes imposed by his own reason upon his own will. Or again the more abstract hypotheses of reason by itself, or will by itself; or again of reason stripped of consciousness, but in intimate conjunction with matter; or of unconscious will in the same combination. Or again the hypothesis of a *tertium quid* between, or compounded of, matter and consciousness, such as we may suppose to be aimed at by the term Mind-stuff. But then we are not restricted to hypotheses of this sort. As the question is now raised, a scientific solution would be all-embracing and final, if it could show anything, no matter what, constant and permanent in the whole, by scientific analysis of the whole into its parts and their relations *inter se*, or in other words could discover a law, or combination of laws, to which the whole in all its parts and all its processes was subject. Consequently it would appear, that a solution is at least conceivable under this third rubric, which if attained would at once be the utmost limit of knowledge, and mark the utmost boundary of existence, and therefore be a bar to all further speculation.

But the foregoing argument overlooks one important fact in the total panorama of the object-matter, which is fatal to its conclusiveness. It omits to notice the elasticity, the fluctuation, in the limits of the panorama. It treats the panorama with its objects as a whole, not only in the sense that no question of genesis can be asked concerning it, which is true, but also in the sense that it is a definite whole, with circumscribed limits, which is false. The panorama, as actually experienced, is always being added to at one end, and vanishing out of consciousness at the other. We never have anything but a portion of it before us at once, and never find any portion definitely circumscribed and isolated, or without what may be called a penumbra where it fades into unconsciousness at either end. We may recall indeed into a single view whatever has once actually passed through the moment of distinct perception; that is, we may treat as a circumscribed total the whole, as well as any part, of past experience; but we cannot so treat what is to come, not even the content of the next future moment. The future escapes inclusion in the ideal scientific solution, and yet the future, just as much as the past, is part and parcel of the whole panorama in the largest sense of the term. The ideal scientific solution would be conceivably final, if the whole panorama, in the largest sense, could be treated like a lake, instead of being treated like an indefinite portion in the course of a river, or if the Universe, which is its object thought of, could be regarded as a molecule enormously magnified, or as a conscious being with powers enormously intensified.

Now this circumscription and isolation of objects is an essential part of the method of science. Its concrete real conditions must be taken as rounded off totals, since otherwise they would be mere elements, aspects, or some other sort of abstraction. Science inherits this view no doubt from common sense, on which it stands and out of which it rises, just as philosophy stands on and rises out of common sense and positive science taken together. But it not only inherits, it also adopts and works with it. And therefore its method can result in nothing else than a conception of the Universe itself as a rounded off and self-contained total, relative indeed in all its parts to knowledge, but in contradiction with the fact, that knowledge is incapable of a similar circumscription. This it is which forbids any ideal solution, conceivably to be attained by scientific methods, being conceived as a final one, even when science is incorporated into a philosophical system, and works in harmony with philosophy, as it is enabled to do by laying aside the conception, that its rounded off and concrete existents are absolute existents.

There is, then, a department or place in philosophy, for questions of a different kind from any that we have contemplated hitherto, questions concerning the nature of the limits of existence as known, or of existence and our knowledge of it taken together. We have to see, if possible, how our knowledge has been enlarged hitherto, or may be enlarged hereafter, by accretions arising, not from further investigation of what we have already got some hold of in general outline, by analogy, anticipatory imagination, or some kind or other of symbolisation, but from what is unknown, or future in respect of knowledge, altogether. In a word, the nature of the limits between the known and the unknown is what we have to see, and whether from this we can infer anything concerning the unknown as such, or as contradistinguished from knowledge.

In order to do this, we must take up the question of the nature of perception, or of percepts, in their lowest terms, their *ne plus ultra* of simplicity, abstracting from everything but their most essential and indispensable features. We must go back to that point in our system, where our second rubric originates out of our first, and ascertain, if possible, the whatness, nature, or content, of percepts simply as perceived, irrespective of their place among, or relation to, other percepts; that is, go somewhat more closely into the analysis of that total object of perception, which we have already distinguished into the two obverse aspects named respectively *objective thought* and *object thought of*. We have distributed this content differently in the third rubric from its distribution in the second rubric. But it does not follow, because these two distributions are co-extensive and cover one another, that therefore no other distribution can be made.

We have now to see something more of the nature of the moment of perception itself, abstracting from the relations, reciprocal or other, between those particular objective thoughts, or percepts, which have at any time passed through the moment of perception. We have to see the connection between what has passed through that moment, what is passing through it, and what is, at that moment, at once future in respect of its genesis into experience, and as yet unknown in respect of knowledge. It is from this analysis that we must derive our conception of the position of our positively known and positively knowable world towards the unknown world surmised beyond it. The analysis when made will take its place in, and be an enlargement of, our total panorama of objective thought; but inasmuch as it will tell us how we must think of a world otherwise unknown, a world beyond the world of positive science, and wholly unknowable by its methods; and inasmuch as whatever we think of that unknown region will be a construction of thought, though a construction made by means of analysis of what is given in the known region; the name for our next and final rubric must be one which makes this new feature of construction prominent. Its name must mark the fact, that its problem is no longer analysis or investigation of a given object-matter, but construction out of previous analysis and investigation.

D

The Constructive Branch of Philosophy.

In entering on a rubric entitled *constructive*, the first question must be,—what becomes of our guiding principle of method, the distinction between nature and genesis? It might seem at first sight to fail us altogether. And it is true, that its practical aid as a guiding distinction is not at first needed; but why? Because in this region, where we have, at first starting, but one single object before us, namely, the object of perception *qua* perceived, filling the whole field of mental vision, no question of genesis is possible, and we are perforce restricted to analyse the object for its nature alone. The construction itself occupies the place of the question of genesis. For the conception of the unknown or unperceived comes directly out of that analysis. In this respect it is like the conception of genesis itself, and the other relations discovered in, and primarily falling under, the second rubric, all of which, being relations between parts of knowledge which have positive content, such as condition and conditionate, whole and part, similar and dissimilar, fail us here, where we come to the object of perception in its lowest terms, or in a form which is involved in, and pre-supposed by, all the rest.

We are familiar with the idea, that an unknown region, something unknown, is implied in the fact of all finite knowledge, or in other words, that finite knowledge reveals something unknown beyond itself; which is in fact only saying over again that the knowledge is finite, or is bounded by what, for the present at any rate, is not knowledge but ignorance. That light reveals both itself and darkness, is a particular case of this more general fact, that knowledge reveals the existence both of itself and of ignorance, that is, of the unknown. If it did not, it would be, not merely knowledge, but unbounded or infinite knowledge, that is omniscience. The root and source of this general fact is what we have now to investigate; and if we find it in the analysis of objects perceived, simply *qua* perceived, the necessary connection of this fourth rubric with those which precede it will be made apparent, and at the same time the class of questions which it contemplates will be marked out.

Generally it may be said (though time forbids me to go into greater detail this evening)*—generally it may be said, that the rubric depends on the nature of the limits between knowledge and ignorance, and embraces all questions which connect a theory of the Universe in its entirety with a theory, or distinct perception, of those limits; or which, in other words, include the region which is wholly beyond positive knowledge in their purview. The well known "Agnoiology" in Ferrier's *Institutes of Metaphysic* may be regarded as an introduction to the whole subject. But to look somewhat more nearly at the questions which it embraces, it will be found, if I mistake not, that it is in this region, which I place under the rubric of the *Constructive Branch of Philosophy*, that systems of Absolute Idealism have their being, that on these heights only are they met, and here alone can they be criticised; I mean systems which are not merely absolutist and monistic, but idealistic also. Hegel for instance, the greatest master, certainly in modern times, of this line of thought, constructs the Universe out of an analysis

* The part below in brackets, from *On the present occasion* down to *infinite existence*, was omitted in delivery.

of objects perceived or thought of, simply as perceived or thought of. Under the same head will come also, I believe, though on this I speak with great diffidence, the three chief systems of Hindu philosophy, in which those ideas are formulated, which underlie both the Brahminical and the Buddhist religions.* In the next place, as already said, it is in this region of thought that the conception first arises of an infinite Universe, as distinguished from a World of possibly finite but indefinitely known circumscription; the term *infinite* meaning whatever has, from the nature of the case, not only no knowable, but also no possible limits, or in other words is known to be unlimited. Finally it is in this region that the question concerning the nature of God, the Object of Religion, arises. A First Cause, whose existence should be conceived merely as a solution of the problems of our third rubric, would, at best and highest, be nothing more than a Demiurge, to whom the attribute of Infinity, which is essential to all religious feeling, must be denied.—These are the main problems, the main controversies, which fall under the present fourth rubric. Their closely similar and at the same time special nature seems imperatively to require some special department of philosophy to be assigned to them. Indeed, it is with questions of this nature, in the opinion of many persons, that philosophy itself begins, and consequently it is on these that, in their opinion, the solution of all other questions depends. These alone, with their immediate consequences, they reckon philosophical. The whole subject matter of my two first rubrics they set down as mere psychology, with which philosophy proper,—which nevertheless includes what I should call an *a priori* psychology,—has little or nothing to do. We have, however,

* See *Dialogues on the Hindu Philosophy comprising the Nyaya, the Sankhya, and the Vedant.* By the Rev. K. M. Banerjea. Williams & Norgate. 1861.

already seen how the present rubric grows out of those preceding it, grows spontaneously as it were, and by the mere application of our principle of method.

[On the present occasion, however, a discussion of these problems would be out of place. I can enter on them only to such an extent as may be requisite to secure the ground of this fourth rubric, by showing that its questions are not mere logomachies, but that the possibilities which it contemplates have a real ground in knowledge as possibilities, and must therefore have some special place or other, within philosophy, appropriated for their discussion. We found the methods of the third rubric inadequate to deal with the solution of the unknown to knowledge, and yet leading those who followed them exclusively to identify the unknown with the non-existent, by a sort of foregone conclusion. The question therefore is, what light is thrown by knowledge itself, taken simply as knowledge, on this relation? We once more have recourse to the strictly subjective method of philosophy, while keeping steadily in view the concrete and positive nature of that known existence, which is one member of the relation to be examined.

We go back accordingly to our first philosophical starting point, and endeavour to make another analysis of the object or content of that kind of perception which has been characterised as primary, under our first rubric. Primary Perception was there described as being virtually though not consciously reflective; that is, as being reflective perception which does not as yet perceive its own reflective character. It has nevertheless a content or object perceived; that is, a content which is characterised as *object* in the secondary or properly reflective perception, which supervenes upon the first or primary perception. To this extent its analysis has been given under our first rubric, where it was said, that the two aspects, objective and subjective, are together the object of secondary or distinctly reflective perception, of that kind of perception which perceives both a content and the fact that this content is perceived, which latter fact is the objectivity of the former, its *thatness* or existence for perception. It was this analysis of the content of primary perception, as the total object of reflective, which was then followed out in the second and third rubrics.

But we have now to enquire, whether this same content of primary perception has not another analysis, besides the analysis which shows it as the object of reflective perception, that is, besides its duplication or distinction into the two obverse aspects, objective and subjective, and also besides that analysis of it into elements, which belongs to the second rubric. We have in fact to see, whether we can or cannot help making another analysis of it as a whole, different from its analysis as a whole into obverse aspects, in which it is taken as the object of reflective perception, as well as different from the analysis of its subjective aspect, *objective thought*, into elements, of which our second rubric gave a general sketch. It does not in the least follow, because we have analysed this content in one way, that we cannot analyse it again in another. It may be capable, for aught we know, of many different analyses, the first being necessarily the analysis of it as a contributory to the moment of reflective perception, which is the moment of experience, the moment of distinct consciousness, the moment in which we first lay hold of anything as an object at all; and which was the moment sketched in our first rubric. The filling up or content of this reflective moment of experiencing anything is and must be concrete, that is, of such a nature as only to disclose its wealth under repeated examinations.

Let us then take any object whatever of reflective

perception, and in thought strip from it everything which it requires a special act of attention for us to be aware of, thus both isolating it from its context in the actual stream of thought, and abolishing all distinct contrasts within itself. We shall then find, that the minimum to which we come in the process, before reducing the object to zero, is a positive content, present to consciousness, having some undefined duration, and in contrast to two *vacua*, one preceding and the other following it, both *vacua* being perceived, that is, being states of consciousness at all, only in attendance upon, and in contrast with, the positive content between them. If *it* was not there, *they* would not be there; if *it* is there, *they* must be. And the only way we have to describe the positive content of this total percept is by some such words as *That! There!*

Now this description is applicable to the residuum or minimum in consciousness of any object of reflective perception, whatever its complexity, extent, or magnitude, from a single presentative sensation to the thought of the entire universe. The total of the residuum or minimum is always, if described subjectively, that is, by reference to the threshold of consciousness, a *minus, plus, minus;* if objectively, or as a content, a *nothing, something, nothing*. The transitions between these moments, that is, between the *minus*, the *plus*, and the *minus*, or between the *nothing*, the *something*, and the *nothing*, require no special act of attention to be perceived, but are part and parcel of the total content. And, what is most remarkable, the *something* comes in between the two *nothings*, and is the *first in order of knowledge*, since they are known only in contrast with it, while *in order of existence* the *something*, the positive portion, seems to come second, following one *nothing* and preceding the other. It is as if it were a single gleam of light falling on some dark pre-existing stream, which save for that gleam would be invisible.

The facts which I have thus given as the analysis of the percept in primary perception are those which Hegel lays at the basis of his system. At least, in attempting to bring his views into comparison with my own, and measuring them so to speak by my own standard,—which is, I suppose, what every one must do, who tries to form an independent judgment of another's theory,—I cannot avoid thinking, that these facts are his basis, analysed of course in a somewhat different way. He took, I imagine, these facts as his ultimates, but at the same time identified the object which I have described as a positive between two negatives (which is in a certain sense a process, since it has duration differentiated into former and latter states), with the process of secondary or reflective perception, which has this process as its object. Whereby the object, *minus, plus, minus,* or *nothing, something, nothing,* becomes, not only a process of consciousness simply, but a process of consciousness, a process of thought, and a process of real genesis in the object, all in one ; a process, moreover, having its principle of movement within itself, the principle of moving by negativity or contradiction, which is a logical principle, or principle of thought. Hegel thus identifies the energy or motive power in things perceived with the logical law of thought perceiving them, and thus it is that his system is a system of Absolute Idealism. The principle of Causality, which Kant laid at the basis of his system, but at the same time left unanalysed, Hegel thus resolves into an attribute of Thought. Thinking is with him the only action; the only real *deed* is *thought.*

The lowest terms in which the Universe is expressible are accordingly, for Hegel,—*Seyn, Nichts* [or *Nichts, Seyn*], *Werden, Etwas ;* or the passage of something without content into something with content. And the whole Universe, in its utmost comprehensiveness and complexity, is embraced by the theory, because the unknown or negative parts in the total object of primary perception are not, as on my analysis, left always outside its positive content, as an unknown Beyond, but are included within it, as parts essential to its composition and movement. Hegel thus constructs the entire Universe out of the indispensable and necessary features of an object in its lowest terms, abstracted from its context in actual experience, but in close union with reflective perception, of which it is an object. In other words, he constructs the entire content of my second and third rubrics out of the analysis which I suppose him to make of the content of my first rubric, the essential results of that analysis being two, first the identification of energy with thought, and second the inclusion of the unknown within the boundary of the known. Hence the Universe comes out not only as an Universe of Thought, an universal Mind, but as an Absolute, or rounded off and self-contained total, just similar in this respect to the Universe as it would be conceived, if a final solution attained by methods of positive science, if such a solution were really attainable.

But to return to our own analysis. It will be observed, that we have obtained our object of primary perception reduced to its lowest terms, in which it seems to me like an island on a sea of nothingness, by consciously abstracting and isolating a concrete object from its context in the actually experienced stream of thought or consciousness. An actually experienced is does not come between two *nothings*, or between two other states of consciousness with positive content. At the same time it is true that we do come, or must come, in the same way to the stream of actual experience that is, the whole panorama of objective thought in its largest sense, in which it includes the whole series or system of real conditions as its object thought of, so soon as we begin to think of it as a total. It too rises out of unconsciousness, and ends in unconsciousness again, and that not only in its historical existence as the experience of an individual's lifetime, but also as the objective correlate of that experience, the real world of existence, of which the historical individual, with his consciousness, is a part.

The whole Universe, thought of by an individual conscious being, can only be thought of by him as seen from within and not from without. He cannot see its limits, he cannot see the context, so to speak, of his panorama as a whole, as we see the context of any particular object, either in the real world, or in the stream of consciousness as it actually occurs. This is a simple fact, the reason for which is partly at any rate psychological, and is indicated by the distinction stated at the end of the last paragraph. It is not because the panorama as a whole is built up out of ultimate percepts, each of which has an atmosphere of negation or nothingness round it,—for this is not the case,—but because the total panorama of real existence is conditioned, for the individual Subject, by the way in which it is brought before him in his actual experience, that is to say, by a process of experiencing which is always going on during his lifetime, and is always incomplete, the past being always in process of vanishing, and the future always in process of appearing.

Abstraction from a context, which we perform artificially in the case of particular objects, is performed for us perforce by nature in the case of the whole panorama, including the order of real conditioning, so soon as we begin to think of it as a whole. For us it is bounded by unconsciousness historically, at the beginning and end of life, and as a panorama by ignorance both at its beginning and end, when thought of historically, and at all those points, or facts, of its content, for which we can give no reason, but must accept as facts, and which from that circumstance we call *ultimates*, when thought of analytically. In short, the Universe, as positively known to us, both when we have reduced it to its lowest terms in thought, that is, to the least number of its simplest ultimate *data*, and also when we have amplified it to its largest knowable extent and complexity of content, is for us precisely in the position of an object of primary perception, of which we can only say *That!* and *There!*

The result is, that the conception of the Universe, as composed of a positive content bounded by the Unknown as by an atmosphere, is a true conception; that is to say, is the only conception of it which harmonises with all the known facts, and other conceptions known to be true. To whatever limits we amplify the positive content of our panorama, it is always bounded by an atmosphere of the unknown. And we mark this difference between the positive but indefinitely elastic content of knowledge and the same content surrounded by its atmosphere, the infinite unknown, by calling one the total panorama of positive knowledge, which is its name as a system of objective thought, and the known (or positively knowable) world, or part of the universe, which are names for it as object thought of; while for the other we reserve the name of the Universe simply.

But if this be so, the question immediately and inevitably occurs,—How, then, is it possible to make any construction of the totally unknown region beyond the limits of the positively knowable, limits which include (be it noted) the penumbra of unexplored phenomena, or facts which may at any time fall within the cognisance of positive science, and which would be embraced by its ideally final solution, spoken of above, supposing such a solution were attained? For not only can we have no facts or phenomena to build with, but our positive conceptions of positive relations, which belong to the panorama of objective thought, are one and all, as it seems, inapplicable here. There is left only the positive conception of Being, and that defined merely by the bare conception of *Percipi*, its own subjective aspect, inasmuch as we have the infinite unknown as an object of reflection, an abstract object without positive content. What real difference is there after all, it must be asked, between what is always, totally, and necessarily unknown, and what others frankly and boldly call the *Unknowable?*

The answer is twofold, if the method which I am following be correct. First, the Unknown is known as *infinite*, which is to some extent a construction of it; and secondly, it is known as *continuous* with the known or positively knowable, notwithstanding that our positive knowledge breaks off sheer with given ultimate *data* in one direction, and with their imagined ultimate results in the other; which is again a construction to a certain extent. We have in fact some sort of hold even of the unknown "Beyond," by the mere fact that it is thought of by us at all, that it is a percept, *percipitur*, or is an object of reflective perception, notwithstanding that we cannot conceive either its reality, or its relation to the known, under any of the positive relations which belong to the analysis of the positively known panorama. Compared with all these relations, its reality, as an object defined by the *percipi* simply, is, to use a favourite Neoplatonist term, ὑπερούσιος.

But the consequences which flow from these two points of construction, the infinity of the unknown Beyond, and its continuity with the known, are not unimportant. Some of these and the bearing of them I will endeavour to indicate as briefly as possible. These two points, it must be noted, are known facts, that is, belong to the reality of the unknown as we must think of it, or as objective to us. So far as they are concerned, we know the real nature of the unknown, just as we know the real nature of objects within the positively known region, within the panorama, within the world of common sense and positive science; —a circumstance which forbids our characterising the unknown as transcendent, or as a world of Things-in-themselves. They are at the same time a construction derived from analysis of given experience, a construction which forms the basis or foundation of further constructions. And these further constructions also must, like them, be derived from analysis of the given; but they are constructions which, unlike the first, we are not compelled by the analysed facts to make, as constructions of the unknown; which therefore we are not justified in attributing to the unknown, as belonging to its real objectivity, or as forming part of its real and known nature. They are thoughts by which we endeavour to represent a reality, which at the same time we know to be really beyond the reach of representation by any such thoughts.

It follows that, in speaking of the Unknown Beyond, we are in this singular position. We are compelled to use terms and phrases drawn from our positive knowledge of the world within the panorama of objective thought, which yet we know are not applicable to the reality of that to which we apply them. Except the three terms, *Real Existence*, *Infinity*, and *Continuity with the Known*, which express known facts concerning the otherwise Unknown, all the terms which we use concerning it are drawn from something which is special, not universal, in experience, and therefore are only figuratively applicable to the Unknown. But it does not follow from this, that all are either alike applicable or alike inapplicable to it, in this figurative sense. The latter of these consequences would be the case, not only with these figurative terms, but also with the three terms which, as it is, are really applicable, if the Unknown were strictly an Unknowable, or wholly out of experience. All terms would then be inapplicable alike. This is an important difference. The terms, if any, which we may find applicable to the unknown infinite, will therefore be rather names of the directions in which we are to place, or the analogies under which we are to conceive, its real attributes, than names describing those attributes themselves. They will be names of relations between positive realities within our own knowledge, standing for realities which we know not positively, but only as having analogous relations to the object of our positive knowledge as a whole. But there is a wide difference between such knowledge of the unknown infinite as this and an absence of knowledge altogether.

Let us see, then, in the first place, what it is that we are doing, in distinguishing the unknown from the known at all. We are taking the universe analytically, and distinguishing one part of it, the whole panorama including all real conditions, as the known, from the rest as the unknown. The whole universe is thus taken as real in both the senses of *reality* defined in my fourth Address, that is, both as a percept simply and as belonging to the order of real conditioning. But while the known part contains known real conditions, and among them the real conditions of our perceiving the existence of the unknown, it is uncertain whether the unknown part contains anything which may be figuratively, but with substantial truth, called a real condition of the known, or not. It may be merely the conditionate of the known, though real as an object of reflection; it may, like consciousness itself, be conditioned proximately on the existence of the Subject, without having in it any existent which is a real condition, as well as a conditionate, of the known with which it is continuous.

At the same time it is clear, that the unknown is placed by thought, relatively to the known, in the *position* at least which would be occupied by a real condition of it, inasmuch as it is necessarily thought of as preceding and surrounding it, as well as following and depending on it. The known or positively knowable part of the universe is bounded by the unknown or ignorance, first, at all points or facts which are ultimate *data* of knowledge, secondly, at all points or facts which mark out its largest conceivable limits in extent and complexity. Its ultimate *principia* in knowledge, and their ultimate consequences or results in knowledge, are alike in contact or continuity with the unknown; that is, at those points, or with those facts, it ceases to be positively known or knowable to us, and our ignorance begins. But does our ignorance conceal what, if we could know it positively, we should know as the real condition of what we now know, or think of as knowable, positively? Is there some unknown form of what we call, in the known world, *Agency, Power, Efficiency?* For again it must be repeated, we cannot know the unknown as a real condition of the known, in the strict sense of *real condition*, because this would not only be knowing *more* of it than the three predicates named above (the possibility of which in some sense is what we want to know), but it would be in contradiction with one of them, namely, *infinity.* For to know anything as a real condition is to know it definitely and positively, that is, as a finite existent.

Now if at this point we look back to the conclusion reached at the end of our third rubric, we shall find that this question is the very one which the scientific method failed to answer, the very one for failing to answer which it was shown, that any solution, which might conceivably be attained by the methods of science, could be regarded only as a partial solution in philosophy, and not as a complete and final one. The scientific view of things, adopted in our third rubric, transformed what, in our second rubric, were called *objects thought of* into *objects thought of as real conditions*. And we found that no definite real condition, or definite law among real conditions, could be conceived, which should be an adequate explanation of the infinity involved in what was there called the elasticity of knowledge. For that would imply the contradiction of the real condition, or real law, proposed as a solution, being thought of as definite and infinite at once. Consequently, in carrying over into the present fourth rubric the final problem bequeathed by the third, the problem of the Real Condition of or in the whole infinite Universe, taken as infinite, is the real question carried over. And what we have been doing in the present rubric, up to this point, is arriving at this same question from the subjective or strictly philosophical side, namely, by analysis of percepts simply as perceived.

The present question, therefore, which is the chief question of the present rubric, is this,—whether we can truly think of the unknown as containing anything analogous to real conditions which act and re-act upon the known? Is there, or is there not, in the unknown, not only a reality for thought, which can be modified as thought by the Subject, but a reality upon which the known and positively knowable world, or any part of it, depends, and which is also modified by the known world in its turn, as consciousness depends upon and is modified by the Subject, or as the Subject depends upon, modifies, and is modified by, the material conditions of its existence?

The great question of the present rubric being thus stated, I would next remark, that the sole interest which man has in imagining or reasoning about the unknown is of a practical kind. He would have a speculative interest in it also, namely, that of acquiring knowledge for its own sake, if it were possible for him to acquire it. But so soon as he sees, that his positive knowledge of it as a reality is restricted to the three predicates which have been named (real existence, infinity, continuity with the known), his speculative interest in the question ceases, because it is evident that no positive or demonstrable answer is to be attained on any terms; and he pursues his speculation solely for the sake of the light which those three predicates may throw back upon his knowledge of the known or positively knowable world, including that of his own mysterious nature, the action or conduct in which it displays itself, and the destiny which may possibly await it in the unknown future. The continuity between the known and the unknown is a real relation between them; and, since he knows himself as the proximate real condition of his own knowledge, he already in one sense knows the unknown as a conditionate of himself, seeing that it is a part of that knowledge which wholly depends for its existence as consciousness on his own existence. *Ignorance* is the name for it as forming part of consciousness. Its name as object thought of is the *Unknown*. But is he to make his ignorance the measure of existence? Can he ignore the possibility, that the unknown may contain *more* than he knows it as containing, that is to say, may be *more* than the vacuity surrounding his panorama? It is evident that his ignorance no more necessarily exhausts the possibilities of its objective aspect, the unknown, than his perception of any positive object, at any given time, necessarily exhausts the positive properties, which on further examination it may be found to contain. He has, therefore, reason to suspect, .that, as he would be intellectually dull, if he ignored the fact of a real relation existing, so he would be practically foolish, if he neglected the possibility, that the unknown may contain agencies which actually affect his own destiny in the unknown future, through the medium of his own action and conduct in the present known world, over which alone he has a determining power. There is, however, a great difference between the two things. The real relation is demonstrable, and must be admitted by all; the real agencies, not being demonstrable, can if we choose be neglected. The one is a matter of speculative notoriety, the other a matter of personal choice, which each individual must decide for himself, and in which no one can prescribe to another.

Once more, then, let us go back to our analytical point of view, which we have quitted for a moment in speaking of a destiny in the unknown future. The whole of known or positively knowable existence may be once more likened to that famous shield which, with its gold and silver sides, has served so frequently and so well in philosophic warfare. This time it is its solid substance and orbicular outline to which I look for aid. The gold and silver sides, that is, the subjective and objective aspects of existence, are both included in that which I now use the shield to represent, namely, the whole known and knowable part of the universe, including all known and positively knowable real conditions. But I no longer use the sides to represent those obverse aspects. The whole shield, as it advances to the front, moves forward in time into the unknown future, to meet and experience its destiny, to make its fortune in what is, historically speaking, unknown. That is an unknown in order of historical genesis; the unknown *a parte post;* and there is also an historical unknown at its earliest imaginable or conceivable commencement, an unknown *a parte ante*. But it is not this historical unknown, either at the knowable beginning or at the knowable end, that we are now concerned with, but with that unknown upon which the destiny of the whole historical future may depend, I mean the unknown in analytical order, the unknown in point, not of genesis, but of nature, the unknown which we picture as lying beyond the utmost circumference of the shield, measuring from its centre; which lies beyond it, not only at any one time or epoch of its history, or advance in historical order, but at all times of its history; which closes round it at whatever time in the past we may conceive its history as a shield, that is, as a positively knowable world, to have begun; and which will close round it again, at whatever time in the future we may conceive its historical existence to terminate.

The whole orb of the solid shield, bounded by the surfaces of its circumference and of its two sides, represents the nature of the known and positively knowable real world, containing objects which are real conditions as well as conditionates. The side surfaces we may picture as covered by a minute mosaic, to represent the analysis of its real nature; the backward-facing surface depicting its nature as it springs out of the past, the forward-looking surface its nature as it enters on the future; and the solid content, which connects portions of the opposite surfaces with each other, standing for individual existents in their character of real conditions. These solid portions of mosaic, which have both a forward and a backward looking surface, we may imagine also as arranged in order of increasing complexity in structure and function, beginning from the centre, so that those which stand for men would occupy the outer circle of the shield, where it was bounded by the circumference. Every solid portion of the mosaic is a real condition. And every individual human being may well feel, as he advances with the rest of mankind, and with the whole world of Nature, organic and inorganic, into the unknown future, that on his own action, at every present moment, the real conditioning of his own future chiefly depends, and also to some extent that of his race, though in an infinitesimal and almost inappreciable degree.

For every individual shares in a nature which, so far as he positively knows, is the highest and most complex of all real existences. He is therefore a being whose nature, analytically speaking, is in contact and continuity with the unknown regarded in its nature, be that nature what it may; a circumstance which we have figured by his place in the shield. In other words, the human nature in which he shares, if estimated and placed in the order of *value*, which is part of the analytical order, is the crowning achievement of Nature as a whole; there is no positively known nature above it, either in moral worth, or in complexity of organisation. He is moreover, in the action of every present moment, moving on into, and contributing to condition, the historically unknown future. The question is, whether in that action he is contributing also to condition the unknown, which we figure as lying beyond and around it, and as necessarily continuing to exist, supposing the historical existence of the known and positively knowable world, including himself, to close and cease? Is a real destiny possibly awaiting him in *eternity*, a destiny which his own action in the present world may contribute to determine?

One more preliminary remark must be interposed, before we quite let go our illustration of the shield. It is necessary to be clear as to what belongs to the real problem, and what belongs to the imaginary illustration. The whole known and positively knowable world, which is imaged by the shield, and is an object thought of, and is real in the second sense of *reality* (inasmuch as it is itself the order of real conditioning, so far as that order is positively knowable), exists in space. But the objective thought, in and by which we know it, when taken in the same reference to the order of real conditioning, and therefore taken in the same second sense of *reality*, exists primarily in time only. That is to say, it exists in space only as dependent on a real existent, the Subject, which is part of the object thought of. Now our problem is concerning the relation between the world, which is the object thought of, and the unknown beyond it. We do not know that it has *space* beyond it. Whether it has or not, is part of the problem of the Unknown. Whatever can be positively figured as existing in space, and all figurations of space itself, even if belonging to dimensions of space other than the well known three, belong, if not to the known, at least to the positively knowable world, which is that penumbra of unexplored phenomena already spoken of, and which we may figure, if we will, by a fringe or halo, attaching like an atmosphere to the circumference of the shield in our illustration.

Accordingly, when we speak of the unknown as lying *beyond*, and as being in *continuity*, and at certain points in *contact*, with the known or knowable world, we are speaking of a limit, a continuity, and a contact, in our objective thought of the world; and these features of our objective thought are drawn from that mode of it which we call *space*. It does not follow, that space, as part of the object thought of, lies beyond the known and positively knowable world, or in other words, that the unknown part of the Universe is spatial. We know it as ignorance in continuity with knowledge. It is within our objective thought, but beyond the object *positively* thought of. Our problem is, whether in *this* unknown, which is not even known as spatial, we have grounds for inferring anything analogous to real conditions, which are conditions of the existence of the known. Now our illustration tends t make us forget this circumstance, by figuring the shield as surrounded on all sides by space. It necessarily figures it so, because it is a part of our objective thought, and is employed to picture the known world, which as object thought of is spatial, but of which we do *not* know, as we know of the shield, that it has space beyond its own limits, or in other words, that it does not share the infinity which belongs to space as a mode of objective thought, while itself being an object thought of.

Another point which the illustration of the shield tends to obscure is the following. The ignorance in our objective thought, which has the unknown for its object thought of, is ignorance, or a blank, in the process of thinking; the infinity of the unknown, which is its object thought of, is therefore infinity in point of time, not of space. But our illustration of the shield has led us to picture this infinity as an infinity of space, as an unlimited space, surrounding a definite figure, existing for some indefinite portion of time. It leads us therefore to mistake the duration of the known and positively knowable world for the duration of time altogether; and thereby to exclude from time in its whole generality that unknown portion of the Universe which is infinite, but which it represents under the figure of infinite space. Time really includes the duration of the infinite unknown, with all which it may contain, as well as the duration of the known and positively knowable world from its beginning to its end, wherever these may be taken. The infinity out of which they are carved, again to speak figuratively, is an infinity of time, and this infinity is what is known by the name of *eternity*.

But now to return to our problem, which, as it was last stated, was stated as a question put by an individual to himself concerning his own destiny. In the first place, then, I must observe, that this question, so far as it concerns the agent individually, is only a part of the larger question concerning the whole known world, the whole mosaic of the shield's surface. He can only answer it, as it concerns himself individually, by answering it as it concerns the whole. Taken merely as it concerns himself, it is but the point at which, or the instance in which, the question concerning the whole is brought under his immediate inspection, or at which he is called upon to form a judgment, one way or the other, about it. In other words, it is a practical and personal question, not because it concerns an individual agent and his destiny only, (for this is not the case), but because he has to give a virtual and implicit answer to it, yes or no, in every distinct choice which he makes between opposite lines of conduct; and therefore, in default of speculative grounds to guide his judgment, his answer must be drawn from motives, or the consideration of motives, which come home to him personally, and the force of which no one can demonstrate to another. His reasons are personal to himself, but the question which they decide is a question concerning the world;—what *he* is to think of *its* real conditions and consequences in the infinite unknown. Are there or are there not real conditions in the unknown, which affect and are affected by those belonging to the known world?

The alternatives attach to actions in their character of real conditions, and therefore the agent cannot escape deciding, merely by refusing to entertain the question as a speculative one. The refusal is itself a decision. Not to entertain the question is practically to answer it in the negative. In acting, therefore, the agent is in reality deciding between the two alternatives of which we have been speaking, besides the alternatives which are ostensibly before him, the two lines of conduct presented to his choice Actions either have, or else have not, real consequences in the infinite unknown world. If, in the case of his own actions, he acts *as if* they had, he virtually chooses the affirmative; if he acts *as if* they had not, he virtually chooses the negative; for he acts in either case on an idea assumed to be true for the purposes of that action. The idea which he entertains and adopts, whether with or without examination, is the rationale or rational justification of his action. Which idea, then, which of the alternative ideas, has he practical grounds for adopting, seeing that all speculative grounds fail him? The overwhelming importance of the affirmative, if it should be true, cannot fail to fix his attention, and compel him seriously to entertain the question, the moment it is seen, that a practical decision cannot be avoided, even by refusing to entertain it speculatively. This is part of what is meant by saying, that the question is a practical and personal one.

But there is something more. By the question being practical and not speculative is meant, that it is not primarily a question of what is true, but of what is best; a question of the relative value or worth of the two alternatives. Speculative questions are questions primarily of what is true, and best only because true. Practical questions are questions of choice, and all choice is between a better and a worse. The true is something known, the best is something chosen. And we have seen that, in the present case, all grounds of knowledge fail us. We are compelled, then, since we must decide between two alternatives, and no third course is open, to decide what is virtually a speculative question, since one alternative must be true and the other untrue, by our practical knowledge, our knowledge of which is the best or most desirable of the two.

Now the choice between definite alternatives, especially when they have such large and far-reaching consequences as in the present case, can never be arbitrary; they must always stand in some definite relations, or have some definite affinities, with other known facts or ideas, which enable a rational judgment to be formed about their relative preferability. And there is a function in man, to which all such alternatives are referable, and which decides between them, a function which is the ultimate arbiter or judge of relative worth or value in every case of choice, both as respects the things to be chosen from, and as respects the volitions and actions in which choosing consists and is carried out,—a function which is known as *conscience*. This function is the ultimate judge, because there is no appeal from it to anything else, but only to the same function again, at a future time. And it is moreover a function which is conscious of this its own supremacy, and of the final validity of its own judgments.*

But conscience is no abstract entity; it is merely the name describing the whole person, or conscious being, so far as he judges his own acts in the moment of acting. It is that mode of reflective perception which takes the relative preferability of motives, as they are actually felt, for its object-matter. But since motives are feelings which are difficult to discriminate, and in which a man may easily persuade himself that he really perceives what he wishes to perceive, the essential characteristic of conscience consists in conscious attention to this possibility, in judging the relative preferability of motives; that is, in attention to its own sincerity in judging. All judgments are volitional actions, and therefore conscience is itself an act of choosing the best motives; that is to say, it is choice and criticism of choice in one; though this

* See Butler's Dissertation *Of the nature of Virtue*, appended to his *Analogy of Religion;* particularly the footnote to the first paragraph. And see also his second and third Sermons *Upon Human Nature*.

choice in knowledge may or may not be adopted by a further act of choice, known as the *fiat* of the will, so as to become the motive finally operative in the resulting action. Apart, however, from this further fiat of the will, conscience is still concrete, and may be described as consisting essentially of two elements, knowledge and feeling, combined in an act of judgment felt to have the highest validity attainable at the time.

But why felt to have this highest validity? Because its decision is of a nature to be verified; but verified, not, as in the case of speculative judgments, by facts which may be known from other sources independently of the judgment, but only by another judgment, the same in kind but more mature, of which it is the sole object; that is to say, a judgment in which the conscience reflects upon itself, and judges its former judgments, as judgments simply, or in respect of their *sincerity*, and which combines purer feeling with deeper insight, or in a word possesses more thorough self-knowledge. Every judgment which a man sincerely passes on his own choice, in the moment of choosing, includes the conviction, that it will be affirmed to have been right at the time of choosing, by future judgments belonging to the same function, and possessing the same essential characteristic of sincerity, to whatever higher degree of insight in point of knowledge, or of purity in point of feeling, he may attain. It is in this conviction that his sense of the validity, as distinct from the sincerity, of his present judgment consists. The later of the two judgments will thus be virtually a continuation of the former which it criticises, affirming its validity for the past, but admitting its imperfection for the present, that is, for those circumstances under which the later and more mature judgment has now to determine the agent's onward course.

Conscience then is an exercise or act of judgment,

which can justify its own sense of the validity of its judgments only by assuming its own perfectibility as a function, that is, the possibility of its indefinite advance in insight, which is knowledge, and in goodness or purity which belongs to feeling. And therefore, when the question between the present alternatives comes before it for decision as a practical question, it must necessarily reject the alternative which denies the possibility of that indefinite advance. Conscience can never admit the thought, that a time will ever come, at which the difference between sincerity and insincerity, that is, between right and wrong, in practical choice of feeling and action, will be abolished. But this would be the case, if the two kinds of action, the good and the bad, were alike arrested in their development, by both alike ceasing to exist with the existence of the known world. The opposite thought, that time will make their essential difference more and more prominent, is the one motive power on which conscience depends for enforcing obedience to its decisions, in the face of opposing and distracting inclinations, and for giving that practical efficacy to its acts of judgment *as actions*, without which their validity *as knowledge* would be an empty name. To limit the efficacy is to change the nature of the action of conscience; it would destroy it entirely as the *known* source of *right*, and leave it standing with no other than a *de facto* character. If conscience does not know its own ultimate validity, it must surrender all claim to unconditional obedience as a judge between conflicting inclinations. Kant's undying service to morals and religion consists in having enforced attention to this central point, however much he may have injured its efficacy by making it rest upon a transcendental theory. It follows, that conscience does not confine itself to repeating, what was assumed in putting the question, that its own indefinite advance in perfection *may be* true, but positively enjoins the adoption of that alternative, on which alone it can be affirmed that it *will be* true; which is saying, in other words, that there are real conditions in the unknown world, which affect and are affected by those belonging to the known world.

To avoid a possible misconception, another point must be noted. It must not be thought that the actual validity of judgments of conscience in the present depends on their being verified hereafter by a perfected conscience; for, in order of existence, the present can never be conditioned on the future. Validity means, that the judgment and the choice commanded by it are right *now*, irrespective of actual consequences, that is, whatever the consequences may be, and whether they will have any *de facto* consequences or not. But the validity and the rightness are felt and known as such; are thought and object thought of in one; and this involves the judgment being felt as verifiable, *if* the function were to be perfected, and even if perfected indefinitely. Validity and the sense of validity are for the conscious agent, in the moment of acting, one and the same thing. The one is all that is then known of the other. The perfectibility of the function is an idea which enters into the analysis of the sense of validity, when the question is asked, in what the sense of validity consists, and whether it is to be justified as a true feeling. Then it is that we see, that the idea of validity implies confirmation by a future judgment, and also that this judgment must be of the same nature as that which it judges. Validity is thus perceived to be inherent in the nature of the judgments of conscience, though a distinct act of reflection is required, in the first instance, for the perception. You cannot prove that a choice is right, any more than you can prove that a colour is red. You cannot demonstrate the difference between right and wrong, any more than you can demonstrate the difference between black and white. Yet sense alone does not tell us that it is ultimate and indemonstrable, though as feeling it is immediate and certain; this requires a distinct act of reflection. So also with conscience. A distinct act of reflection is required to justify its sense of validity, and raise it to the rank of a knowledge of validity. Sense and conscience are both ultimate, and therefore ultimately indemonstrable. But there is this great difference, that sense is ultimate in the region of fact simply, while conscience is ultimate in that of choice, and therefore to some extent commands the future, in commanding action. This perception in the case of conscience, when once attained, is incorporated with conscience, as the knowledge which it has of its own validity, that is, of itself as the source of right.

The idea of perfectibility, which is reached and employed, as it were, on the way to this knowledge, is not suggested to reflection by the moral character of the judgments of conscience. They derive this property from a deeper or rather an ampler source, namely, from their being practical judgments, as distinguished from speculative. A few words must be devoted to this point. The end aimed at by every practical judgment is indefinite in its issue or final result, its general outline only being definable, and that definable only by the line taken in initiating it, or as determined by the judgment which decides the immediate action. A practical judgment is one which, by looking back at past experience, decides the direction of the next step forward into the unknown. If a definite end is set before the agent, as the end which he has already resolved to aim at, his judgment is a judgment of means to an end, a comparison of known probabilities, and is to that extent a speculative judgment. Judgments of this kind form a class within practical judgments, a narrower class which may be called *prudential.* They are not judgments of the comparative preferability of ends simply, but only of subordinate ends as means to others, that is, of the relations which certain definable actions bear to ends already known or assumed as relatively final. The solution which they aim at is the solution of some definite problem. In this they resemble all speculative solutions, and though often called practical, and confused with judgments and solutions which really are so in the larger sense of the term, they differ in the essential point now named from those which we have hitherto been speaking of as distinguished from the speculative class, and to which all judgments of conscience belong. Speculative solutions aim at results which are definite as anticipated results, practical solutions at results which are indefinite as anticipated results, though of a definite kind, and yet necessarily assume that the results which they aim at are attainable. They adopt a line of action which they conceive as possibly issuing in a series of real though at present indefinitely known attainments.

Practical judgments, then, simply as such, have a validity of their own, which is, however, nothing more than the promise or hope which every practical choice of a line of action bears within itself, of leading to some real result which will be preferable to the results of an opposite line of action. This forward looking hope is essential to practical choice, and is the characteristic distinguishing it from speculative choice, which affirms only what can be inferred as a fact from actual experience. Both practical and speculative judgments are modes of reflective perception, looking back upon past experience; but while speculative judgments do this with a view to acquire more accurate knowledge of facts considered as already and extraneously determined, practical judgments do it in order to determine new facts, by determining choice of new action. All action as such, that is, as distinguished from feeling and from knowledge, is movement forward in time, and the content of an action, as distinguished from the content of a feeling, or of a knowing, is definable only by reference to the termini which its onward movement connects. All conscious action, therefore, involves a conscious reference to futurity. And in this nature of action, as action simply, lies the ultimate reason why a forward looking hope is necessarily bound up with all conscious choice of action, that is, with all practical judgment.

Perhaps it may be well at this place to recall the fact, that it is here, namely, in the distinction between action as such, from feeling and knowing, that the practical or ethical branch of philosophy has its point of divergence from the speculative branch. This fundamental distinction is part of the general analysis of the elements of consciousness embraced by our second rubric, and thus it is that both branches of philosophy alike have their parent stem in the subjective analysis of consciousness generally, which is speculative philosophy in the wider sense of the term, as both also are alike grounded in the facts of human nature, which are the object-matter of that analysis.

Now conscience, which is itself a form of practical judgment, commands, as we have seen, the adoption of that alternative which affirms, that real conditions in the known world have real consequences in the infinite and unknown world; and it commands its adoption, because it is bound up with its own knowledge of validity as the function of moral judgments, which again is bound up with the felt validity of the function of practical judgments simply. But in this it does not lay aside its own fundamental character of being practical choice between alternatives, or forfeit the promise which every practical choice bears within itself of leading to some indefinitely known result, which will be at once the consequence and the justification of its present action. It is the unknown future to which it looks for the realisation of its hopes, which are inseparably bound up with its practical decisions. Conscience, therefore, in commanding the adoption of the idea, that real conditions in the known world have real consequences in the infinite and unknown world, is in fact ideally projecting itself into, or conceiving an idealisation of itself as really existing in, the unknown world; that is, as having existed indefinitely, and to exist indefinitely, in eternity. For its ideal consists in two things, perfect knowledge combined with perfect goodness; and this ideal, in consequence of its adopting the affirmative idea of real conditions in the unknown, with which idea it is bound up, is thenceforward conceived as effectuated and made actual in eternity by infinite power.

Conscience in its double character, of practical forward looking action and ultimate judgment of right or best action, at once imagines the realisation of its own ideal in the unknown future, and commands the expectation of it as a duty. And inasmuch as conscience is but another name for the highest form of practical judgment which is known to us, there is literally no reason to be urged in favour of the opposite alternative. For this nothing can be urged, unless it be the pleasure of maintaining the absolute origination of existence in time; I mean, of course, the existence of the known and positively knowable world; a creation, by the created, *ex nihilo;* joined with the pleasure of imagining its return *in nihilum* again. Perhaps the force of this motive may be underrated. A good logical absurdity would seem, for some minds, to have all the attractiveness of vice, to be "as' easy as lying," and a good deal pleasanter. Everything which is good in man's nature speaks in favour of the belief, that the unknown is so constituted as to realise and confirm the dictates of conscience. And it may be added, that there are secret springs of energy in human nature, which are unlocked and called forth into activity, only by dwelling on this idea.

On this line of thought we conceive, or rather endeavour to conceive, the Universe as infinite power actuating infinite knowledge and infinite goodness. The combination is impossible to realise in a single thought, since to realise it in thought would be to imagine a single real conscious being, or person, in whom these infinite attributes should be combined, and every single real existent must be thought of as finite. We are therefore unable to consider these attributes as together constituting a single conscious being, by reference to whose nature or action either the nature or the laws of the known world can be explained. Even if the conception were logically possible,—which it is not,—the single conscious being, who would be the object of it, would be finite, and the attempted explanation would therefore be open to the same objection, which was above held fatal to the pretensions of any ideally final solution supposed to be attainable by scientific methods. The combination of the three attributes, of infinite power, knowledge, and goodness, is man's attempt to realise the thought of that infinite and eternal Universe, which he can only see or think of from within, but which he must think of as existing in accordance with his own limited and positive knowledge. In other words, *Reality* (in the sense of real conditioning power) resides, not in an existent formed by the union of these attributes, but in the *Infinite*, of which they are the part intelligible to man.

The reality beyond is power, *and more;* knowledge, *and more;* goodness, *and more;* their combination in a person, *and more.* The reality is man's highest ideal and infinite besides, a Being or a Power which is real, though unimaginable to human thought. This Infinite Reality, laid hold of mentally, rather than conceived, by means of these attributes, and upon which the known and positively knowable world depends for its existence, man has named *God;* trusting it *Faith;* obeying it, in obeying conscience, *Religion.* It is of the essence of religion to rest on faith, not on knowledge. If (*per impossibile*) it rested on knowledge, it would no longer be religion but prudence. All which religion requires from knowledge is a basis on which faith may stand, the perception that there is an Infinite beyond knowledge, involved in knowledge itself.

Thus in result we see, that the problems of the present rubric, the Constructive Branch of Philosophy, escape the grasp of speculation, only to fall within the province of practice, and its highest function of practical judgment, conscience. The Universe cannot be embraced in its whole nature by any speculative conception which man can frame, but man can frame a conception of his own relation to the Universe, or in other words, of what the Universe is to him, at once sufficiently definite, and indispensably necessary, for his practical guidance. The basis of that conception is analytical and speculative, the superstructure constructive and practical. Philosophy begins with knowledge of the seen, and ends with faith in the unseen; knowledge itself testifying that the Universe exceeds its power of intellectual comprehension. The last word of knowledge is faith, the last word of philosophy is religion.

The history of the forms which religion has taken, from the earliest stages known to us in human history to the present day, is a history of the changes in human thought regarding the Unknown Infinite. All such thought is anthropomorphic, that is, it invests some unknown Beyond, surmised as existing or embodied now in one kind of object, now in another, with the attributes of human personality. The devolpment is twofold, consisting in two concomitant series of changes, in combination with and reciprocally affecting each other. One of these is the growth of positive knowledge of natural phenomena; the other the development of human character, and consequent change in moral feeling, as civilisation advances. The stage reached at the present day, which is also necessarily anthropomorphic, is what I have had before me in endeavouring to analyse the train of thought, which connects our positive knowledge with our conceptions of the unknown infinite. Our knowledge has at length reached a point, at which we can clearly distinguish the whole range of positive knowledge, actual or possible, from the infinite ignorance which lies beyond it, and thus make our ignorance itself objective. Accordingly we no longer surmise the unknown Beyond as embodied, or manifesting itself, in objects of any kind, even in those of the highest kind we know of, that is, in men, nor yet in the whole positively known or knowable world; but we conceive it as being the unknown part of an infinite whole, which is pervaded, in both its parts alike, by the attributes under which alone we can lay hold of it in thought. The power or agency in the known world, the *That which* makes, or does, or acts, and which, as we have seen, escapes our positive and scientific knowledge, is thus identified with the infinite power which sustains both worlds, known and unknown, alike, and which, together with the attendant attributes of knowledge and goodness, we conceive as Divine, that is, as a Majesty inhabiting Eternity. It is *this* Beyond, namely, the unknown in our positive knowledge, which we invest with human attributes, acknowledging at the same time, that we do so because it is a necessity of practical human *thought*, and therefore that these attributes are partial and feeble adumbrations of the infinite reality, which both in its infinity, and in its other real attributes speculatively taken, escapes at once the largest grasp and the deepest insight possible to man.

I make this remark on the history of religion, because in the history we again touch the ground of the common-sense world. As with the whole of philosophy, so it is with that part of it which is the philosophy of religion. Philosophy develops out of its own actual history, and at the same time sheds upon its history in retrospect a clearer and clearer light. The history both of philosophy as a whole, and of the philosophy of religion, begins with the common-sense world. It is to that world that all popular religious creeds belong. Standing on grounds of common sense, they are subject to the laws which govern the rise, development, modification, and decay, of beliefs and systems of belief in that domain. It is therefore on the acknowledged footing, that philosophical systems and popular religious creeds belong respectively to two quite different regions of thought, that the relations between them will have henceforward to be judged, and an agreement between philosopher and non-philosopher to be established, concerning the articles of religious faith which are tenable by both in common.

Popular religious creeds are no more abolished, in point of general and substantial truth to reality, by the philosophy of religion, than the common-sense belief in the real objective existence of the material world is abolished, in point of general and substantial truth to reality, by philosophical analysis in its entirety. As an infant, in growing up to childhood, gradually forms his common-sense belief in the external material world, aided by his inherited mental organisation and aptitudes, and by the instruction of his elders, so also, by the same means, and *pari passu,* he gradually forms his common-sense belief in the existence and nature of the Divine. Analogous to both these branches of an individual's entire belief, is the development of belief and knowledge concerning the World and God, in the various races of mankind, and in mankind as a whole, in their progress to maturity. It is at a certain epoch of this development, in the history alike of individuals, of races, and of mankind at large, that philosophy arises; beginning with the first consciously introspective question which a man puts to himself, concerning the nature and validity of his own knowledge. In one sense, it is true, in entering on philosophy he quits the ground of common sense. He quits it as a department of knowledge distinguished from the philosophical department on which he is entering, but not as the experiential basis which all philosophical knowledge pre-supposes. It is that form of experience which is the *explicandum* of philosophy, that indispensable condition without which philosophy would lack, not only a *de facto* or actual, but also a rational or *de jure* existence.

Common sense, science, and philosophy, are three modes of regarding the same Universe, of which science is more profound and exhaustive than common sense, and philosophy more profound and exhaustive than science. Each of the three has its own office and function; each is a supplement, not a substitute for the others. This would not be the case, if any of the three attained or could attain to an *absolute* knowledge, which from its nature must either absorb or abolish knowledge of every other kind. It is common sense which, at the present day, is the most reluctant to renounce this untenable pretension. Philosophy need not fear, in renouncing it, that mankind will ever cease to cultivate a mode of enquiry which is recognised as more profound and exhaustive than other modes, merely because it no longer *professes*, either to be completely exhaustive of existence, give a knowledge of the existent *in itself*. On the one hand, to do the best we can, though it may not be the absolute best, is ingrained in human nature; and on the other, it is of the essence of knowledge to be relative to a knowable, so that, for thought, the *in itself* is the non-existent. The three modes are indeed so many stages on the road towards an exhaustive knowledge of existence; but the road on which they are stages is infinite, and the intervals which lie between their highest several attainments are infinitesimal, compared to the infinite interval by which the highest attainment of the highest of them is divided from omniscience.

One more remark I would make, if I have not already tried your patience too far. The idea which has been occupying us above, that the existence of the Subject may possibly be prolonged into the Unknown, is quite different from the idea of a future life, or immortality, as commonly stated. The known world, which we have now been contrasting with the unknown, includes within itself the positively knowable, which is that portion of it described above, under the third rubric, as a sort of penumbra of unexplored facts within the competence of positive science, a region lying between the final results, which are at any time actually attained by positive science, and the ideally final solution which is conceivably within the reach of its methods. To this region at present belong the questions, first, whether there is or is not a world of immaterial or etherial conscious beings beyond the actually known world, and secondly, whether men, or other positively known conscious beings, may have their life prolonged beyond death, which is the event with which their life in the actually known world closes. In other words, the question of a future life, as a possibly demonstrable reality, and the question of the real existence of a world of spiritual beings other than man, are questions for science, or for the scientific department of philosophy, and not for our present rubric.

The idea, I confess, has frequently occurred to me, building upon the same hypothesis of an etherial medium, which Mr. Knowles has made the basis of his well known theory of brain-waves,* that it may be one function of the nerve and brain organism, while serving as the proximate real condition of consciousness, to build up within itself, and along with its own development, an etherial organism, which, after the death of the grosser organism which is its parent, may be capable of a separate existence under quite different conditions from those at present known to us. And farther, this etherial organism, thus entering on a new life, may be the Subject of a new consciousness, which may retain the memory, and be in fact the continuation, of the consciousness, which, in the present state of existence, is conditioned upon the parent organism. Roughly speaking, this would be to regard the "Soul" as the product, instead of the condition, of the vital and conscious powers of the body. Be this however as it may, if the two questions now mentioned, or either of them, should ever be answered by science in the affirmative, the effect would be to include what is now the positively knowable within the limits of the positively known. But this would in no way alter the relation, now set forth, between the known and positively knowable, taken together, and the unknown Beyond. Wherever the circumscribing limits of the known world are drawn, it is there, and there only, that it is in contact and continuity with unknown and infinite existence.]

* See the *Nineteenth Century* for June 1882 (Vol. xi. p. 900), referring to an earlier paper, in the *Spectator* for Jan. 30, 1869.

III.

SUCH are the outlines of the organic articulation of philosophy as I conceive it, the main divisions into which, in my opinion, philosophy will mould itself, if it is based on experience, and pursued on definite principles of method, that method being dictated by experience alone. I cannot think of any problem which does not readily fall into rank, and present itself for treatment, under some one or more of its four rubrics, so soon as the method of asking first *what*, and then *how comes*, is applied to it. I do not say that every problem can be *solved*, if it is so treated; some problems are insoluble in every shape; others are mares' nests from the first, owing their very origin as questions to misconception. But in every case, the treatment now proposed will show whether a problem is soluble or not, and if the latter, will disclose the grounds of its insolubility. The four rubrics themselves would at least seem to be exhaustive. Under the first, everything is treated simply as present to consciousness. Under the second, everything is analysed for its content. Under the third, everything is examined as to its genesis and behaviour. Under the fourth, the limits of knowledge itself in every respect are brought under discussion.

But quite apart from the question whether this method be the true one or not, a point on which I do not presume to dogmatise, there is another point on which, as President of a Society for the Systematic Study of Philosophy, I am bound to insist. It is this, that the question of method is a vital question, a question of life or death for philosophy, at the present day. Philosophy exists at present in the form of some half-dozen or dozen separate philosophies, each based on principles antagonistic to those of the rest. Moreover this dismemberment of philosophy is progressive, and, unless checked, can issue only in the discredit and virtual annihilation of philosophy in the intellectual world. Now every distinct and autonomous branch of knowledge is defined by two things in conjunction. It must have a distinctive purpose and a distinctive method. The question, then, must be fairly faced by a Society like ours, whether philosophy, as such, has a distinctive purpose and a distinctive method; and this question is vital, not merely for philosophy, but for our Society, the existence of which is justified only by the existence of philosophy as a distinct branch of knowledge. Observe, I do not say, that the method and purpose of philosophy must necessarily be those for which I have been arguing; nor do I say, that they may not ultimately be found in some one of the existing philosophies, which are now striving for exclusive possession of the field. But this I say, that the question, what they are and where they are to be found, is the first and most vital question for us to face, as a Society for the systematic study of philosophy. I hold it an immense advantage, that we admit discussion, and welcome the representatives, of every school and phase of philosophic opinion. Every school must face this vital question. And in laying my own views of method before you, I would have them regarded only as my individual contribution to its distinct enunciation and settlement.

The method which I have described places philosophy, as I venture to think, in an independent and unique position among intellectual pursuits, and raises it to the rank of a definite discipline, aiming at the acquisition of a definite kind of knowledge, in which various students may labour independently, without clashing, and to a common end; may labour not only in different departments, or on different parts of the subject, but at once on the same parts in the same department; the systematic *distinction* of departments being that which secures, not of course agreement in the several analyses made by independent students of the facts before them, but that the facts before them are recognised as the same. It ascertains the sameness or difference of the facts, or sets of facts, which are severally intended by different and independent students, and prevents their speaking of the same facts while thinking them to be different, or of different facts while thinking them to be the same, and thus either affirming or denying the results obtained by one another, under misconception as to what the results really profess to be, and to what part of the subject they belong. And what is perhaps a still greater boon, it permits a student to own himself mistaken, and mistaken in his analysis even of the most important matters, without thereby robbing his whole philosophical work of its value, as it would have been robbed by admission of what must appear, under existing methods, as a flaw in some vital part of his theory.

This could never be the case, nor could there be any room for different and independent workers at the same sets of facts, so long as philosophy was conceived as the attempt to unlock the secret *adytum* of the Universe by the master key of some happily conceived thought, and thereby develop its system from some single truth, by which at once its whole outline was comprehended and its inmost essence penetrated; as for instance, Hegel's conception of Self-creative Thought acting on the logical principle of Contradiction. Still less, if possible, could it be the case, so long as philosophical systems were made to rest on unproved assumptions; as for instance, the scholastic, orthodox, or dualistic assumption of Absolute Mind as the creator of Matter, or on the more refined assumption, made by Kant, of a transcendent Appercipient as the constructor of experience. When Kant proposed the question, *How are synthetic a priori judgments possible?*

CPSIA information can be obtained
at www.ICGtesting.com
Printed in the USA
BVHW081605280119
538839BV00027B/2039/P